VANLIFERS

BEAUTIFUL CONVERSIONS
FOR LIFE ON THE ROAD

EDITED BY
ALEX WAITE

The
History
Press

Front cover: Rob and Emily of theroadisourhome
Page 4: Lisa and Janek of orangeroadtrip

First published 2021

The History Press
97 St George's Place, Cheltenham,
Gloucestershire, GL50 3QB
www.thehistorypress.co.uk

British Library Cataloguing in Publication Data.
A catalogue record for this book is available from the British
Library.

ISBN 978 0 7509 9718 8

Design by Katie Beard
Printed in Turkey by IMAK

CONTENTS

FOREWORD
BY DEE CAMPLING

I'm Dee Campling and I'm an interior designer and stylist. My main inspiration and speciality is the blurring of boundaries between the outdoors and indoors. I love to take the inside outside by treating outdoor spaces as rooms and bringing the outside inside with the colours, textures, forms and materials from nature. Living at one with nature is, as we all know now, so good for your mind, body and soul.

I've also always loved camping and the concept of creating a little home away from home in nature. Over the years we've owned bell tents and a vintage caravan, all of which I've furnished with accessories such as rugs, cushions and proper bedding (never boring sleeping bags!). For me, the delight in creating your own personal and portable holiday home far outweighs staying in often soulless, and always expensive, hotels.

The coronavirus pandemic brought forward our long cherished and saved for plans to move on from tents and build our own campervan. We opened the door to vanlife world and were delighted to discover, via YouTube and Instagram, thousands of stories of people who had already converted all types of vans into mobile living spaces.

VanLifers: Beautiful Conversions for Life on the Road captures eighteen of these inspiring and informative stories, and shows how a person of any age or life stage, with any budget, can create a beautiful, personal campervan. From builders' vans to firetrucks, any vehicle can be converted as long as it's solid and big enough for your particular needs. The vanlifers in this book explain their thought processes, share their design tips and reflect on the parts of their van builds that they're particularly proud of as well as those they wish they'd done differently.

Like the vanlifers in the book, we're realising that the experience of converting a van, and then living in it, brings much more to your life than you originally expected. It really does open up a new world of small-space design and simple living, and the fact that this lifestyle is always centred around nature makes it feel very authentic.

The fascinating stories in *VanLifers: Beautiful Conversions for Life on the Road* capture this authenticity, make me very glad that we've chosen vanlife, and will inspire you to choose it too.

Dee Campling
August 2021

INTRODUCTION

Since motorhomes first appeared in the early 1900s, people have enjoyed taking their creature comforts with them on holiday. VW campers appeared in the 1950s and immediately took off, becoming an iconic symbol of 1960s liberty.

While love for campers and motorhomes is still widespread, converting your own vehicle to live and travel in has become increasingly popular in the UK over recent years – and the coronavirus pandemic has only increased the trend further. Purchasing of commercial vehicles is up by 57 per cent, and searching for #vanlife on Instagram brings up over 8 million posts showing beautiful conversions and tantalising scenes from around the world. There are several Facebook groups devoted to self-builds and life on the road, from traditional vans to rarer ambulance, horsebox and lorry conversions.

Whether your vehicle is intended for living in permanently, for weekend getaways or for once-in-a-lifetime adventures, life on the road can offer an unparalleled sense of freedom, with endless opportunities for new experiences, and joining a friendly worldwide community.

There are lots of companies who can create an amazing home on wheels to suit many different lifestyles, but for many vanlifers the joy is in converting it themselves and making it personal and unique. But creating a home that is unique to you and your needs is always a challenge, even more so when it has to move. As well as considering the layout and size, weight is often an important factor as it affects speed and stability – as well as the licence required to drive it. For some vanlifers, they have to consider more than just their own tastes and needs. Some vanlifers hit the road with their families and have to factor in multiple sleeping areas, while others have furry companions who need to be accommodated and kept safe.

After witnessing the conversion taken on and completed by a friend, I was inspired to gather stories and tips from amazing people around the world who have decided to take on the challenge of a self-build for a wide range of vehicles. In their fascinating, often moving, accounts and beautiful pictures you can see their creativity shining through, particularly in the many ways they have adapted their mobile homes to suit their lives. From storing bikes and climbing equipment under beds to eco-friendly power sources – as well as working out the tricky toilet situation – no two stories or solutions are the same.

Whether you are converting your own vehicle, thinking about doing so in the future or just enjoy imagining a life on the road, their tales and advice are sure to inspire you – they have definitely inspired me.

DRIVING AND SKIVING

Vicki and Stu converted their van, Fleur, so they can enjoy weekend adventures with Ella the dog, enjoying the freedom it gives them.

We're Vicki, Stu and Ella the dog. Our self-built campervan, Fleur, is a 2010 Citroen Relay that we've had since 2014.

We don't live full-time in our van – we're mainly weekend warriors. But we try to draw out those weekends as much as we can, spending a few days here and there working remotely from the van to maximise our free time. We love the freedom and flexibility this gives our lives. We can both do our jobs remotely and we have plenty of power to run our laptops, meaning we can make the most of our evenings and weekends by eliminating the need to travel once we've clocked off for the evening.

We always knew we wanted a camper, but we could never have afforded a coach-built one, so that was a key driver for us in deciding to convert our own. That said, we think there are loads of benefits to self-builds too. We've designed our van around our needs and if we feel that something's not quite working for us, we can change it. We've come to really appreciate the versatility of having a self-built camper. We also like feeling a little less conspicuous than we might do in a motorhome, especially when we're tucking ourselves away somewhere for the night.

We bought Fleur as a bare panel van in 2014. At the time Stu was a full-time mature student, working as an HGV driver at the weekends, and he managed to spend one or two days a week working on the conversion. This big push in the first few months got the van to a usable point, with windows, insulation, electrics, a bed frame and a bench installed. At that point we started using the van regularly and have continued to do so ever since, chipping away at all the other jobs in between trips. We're six years in now and we still can't say it's finished!

We're amateur converters and our DIY skills aren't perfect, but we've got Fleur pretty close to where we want her to be and she's become an integral part of the family.

A lot of research and planning went into the technical aspects of the build, including the windows, insulation, electrics, plumbing and gas. In our opinion, these are the things that you really can't afford to mess up and mistakes can be expensive or even dangerous. We also put a lot of planning into the layout of the space available. We thought hard about how we'd be using the van and what kit we'd be taking with us on different trips. Once these key elements had been planned, we pretty much made the rest up as we went along.

At the beginning, we put very little thought into what the van would finally look like. Our main priority from the outset was that the van worked for us practically, and everything else came second to that.

Since those early days, we've spent a lot of lazy mornings lying in bed, looking around the van and discussing what we'd like to change or add next. The van works well for us, but despite all the discussions and the planning, there are still some things that we'd do differently if we were starting all over again. We guess that just comes with experience!

We paid £6,500 for Fleur when she was a 4-year-old panel van with 95,000 miles on the clock. Because we've spread the expense of the build out over so many years, we've not kept a strict, itemised budget, but we estimate that we've spent about £4,000 on the conversion.

Our biggest outlay was our LPG heating system, which we only recently installed. This came in at just over £1,000, with the under-slung LPG tank and Propex heater costing around £500 each. We did most of the installation ourselves then paid a professional £90 to connect the gas to the heater and test it for us, which was a bargain for the peace of mind it has given us. Our LPG tank also fuels our stove, so that outlay wasn't just for the heater, but we chose the tank capacity based on what we'd need to run the heating for a couple of weeks at a time.

We also splashed out on our fridge, which has a huge capacity and runs very efficiently off our solar system. We picked it up in a sale and managed to get a good discount, but this fridge usually retails at a few hundred pounds.

Some of the interior has helped to offset these big expenses though. Our most satisfying bargain has to be the chest of drawers under our bed. These old, broken melamine drawers were being thrown out by someone, but they were the perfect fit. We fixed them, spruced them up with some leftover furniture paint and built them into place. They now store our clothing, while our dining table stows away in a little hatch above.

We saved some money on other materials too, by using pallet wood for a lot of our furniture when a local warehouse let us take some discarded pallets from their yard. The look of pallet wood isn't to everyone's taste, but we love it and it's saved us a fair amount in timber costs. There are some risks when working with pallets and they can be a pain to break apart, so it's worth doing some research on the dos and don'ts, but they can be a beautiful and cost-effective option. We've seen some stunning van interiors where people far more skilled than us have done very impressive things with pallet wood.

Another bargain was our bench seat in the cab. When we bought Fleur, she had two cabin seats up front and we made the controversial decision to swap out the passenger cabin seat for a double bench seat. The vast majority of

'Having some home comforts to retreat to at the end of the night is priceless. Fleur invariably becomes the party van when we're at festivals.'

self-builders do the opposite, but for us the cab was never going to form part of our living space and we really missed having a third seat. We were able to sell our battered old cabin seat for £200 and pick up a brand-new double bench seat for £30, so we actually made money by adding the extra seat. It's just as well we did, as now that's where we strap in Ella when we're on the road.

We use our van as a travelling studio apartment in pretty much any situation, including visits to family and friends (we've slept on a lot of driveways), but it's mainly a hub for activities. We dabble in a few different sports, which means we have a stupid amount of kit. Over the years, our hobbies have shifted slightly, and we've realised the value of having as much flexible storage as possible.

We never originally intended to build so many lockers, drawers and shelves, but the more we built, the more homely Fleur started to feel. We really appreciate having things organised in cupboards and drawers, instead of living out of plastic tubs and suitcases.

When it comes to sports equipment, we've fitted bespoke shelves under the bed for our mountain bikes and we have loads of storage for smaller kit, like climbing and hiking gear. On the flip side, we've both started surfing recently and, because we never factored in surfboard storage when designing the van, we've had to develop a workaround for that. We travel with the boards in the living space and move them into the cab when we're parked up. It's

not ideal because it's a faff to move them once we've parked up (which can be awkward, especially if we're trying to keep a low profile) and it would be difficult to make a swift getaway if we ever felt we needed to. But it's a reasonable solution and means we don't have to share our tiny living space with two surfboards!

Now we've fitted our heater, we're no longer restricted to staying in places with hook-up points during winter and we're keen to head for the Scottish and European mountains as soon as we can. As well as housing bikes in the summer, the shelving in our garage space was designed to fit snowboards and winter kit too. We can also remove the shelves altogether if we ever need to open the space up for bulkier gear.

As well as being our activity lodge on wheels, our van also comes with us to a few festivals every summer. We both play in bands and our summers tend to be busy, so having some home comforts to retreat to at the end of the night is priceless. Fleur invariably becomes the party van when we're at festivals, so we recently added some dedicated booze storage as an essential upgrade.

So, we've managed to figure out solutions for most of our gear, but we're conscious that our storage solutions aren't perfect. We've seen other conversions which have kit storage factored in beautifully and it's a joy to behold!

Our ultimate aim is to be able to begin working more flexibly, so that we can spend several weeks in the van at a time. We're laying the foundations for this now, but we plan to always have a bricks and mortar base to come back to. We'd ultimately like to be able to pack up the van for a winter in the mountains, head back in spring for a clear out and then repack for summer.

Most of the travelling we've done in the van over the past few years has been in the UK and we really enjoy making the most of what we have on our doorstep. We've taken the van to mainland Europe a couple of times, but we've generally been pretty happy exploring home soil. We're based in the south-west, so Cornwall, Devon, South Wales and Pembrokeshire are regular haunts for us. We've also spent a lot of time in North Wales, Scotland and the Lake District. Once we can get away for longer periods though, it's likely we'll start venturing further afield.

We're due to get married in Snowdonia soon and our van will be our bridal suite. We're planning to drive straight to Scotland from the venue and spend our honeymoon exploring the Highlands with our trusty hound in tow.

○ Follow Vicki and Stu's adventures on Instagram at drivingandskiving and on their website drivingandskiving.com where they have lots of tips for aspiring vanlifers.

FLEUR

Cost of van:	£6,500 purchase
Cost of conversion:	£4,000
Biggest outlay:	LPG heating system
Best savings:	Pallet wood for timber and bench seat in cab
Essential upgrade:	Booze storage for festivals
Future plans:	Honeymoon in Scotland

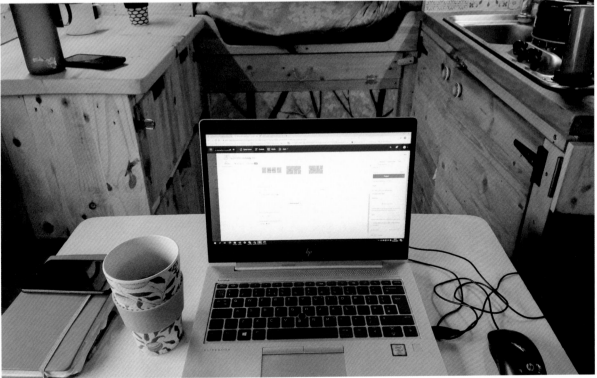

CAMPER DREAMIN'

Izzy and Laurie love all things adventure, both big and small, whether it's van building, road tripping, climbing or hiking with their dog, Bear. They live for the weekends when they can hit the road, lose themselves in the great outdoors and break free from their working weeks.

The Camper Dreamin' story started in 2017 when they picked up an old painter's van and converted her into the ultimate adventure wagon, lovingly known as Yosemite. After many adventures on the road and with a new love of van building, it didn't take them long to dream up their next van and they soon started the next second conversion, now known as The Grizzly.

Our greatest love has always been to travel. Everyone who knows us, knows that we are always planning the next big adventure. Over recent years, the focus of our travels started to be less about new countries and cultures, and more about losing ourselves in the great outdoors. We swapped hostels for campervan rentals, opted for wheels instead of wings, and took to the roads to feed our travel bug. We fell in love with the lifestyle and were instantly hooked!

We started dreaming about having our own campervan, but it always felt like a pipe dream. Then, in 2016, we started climbing. We found ourselves camping most weekends, pitching our tent after a long day on the rock, only to wake up the next morning and take it back down again. Suddenly, owning our own camper moved from ‹pipe dream› to ‹total necessity›, so we decided to just get on and do it.

We don't live in our van full-time, but it is a huge part of our lives. For us it epitomises freedom. Our means to escape everyday life is parked up outside our house, ready and waiting to go at a moment's notice. The moment we turn the key in the ignition at the start of each road trip it's like we are a turning off the pressure of our working lives. With every mile we drive, we can feel our souls coming alive and our batteries recharging. We talk of adventures and happy things, and some of our greatest and daftest plans have come from road trip chats. When we hit the road, we embark on a simpler way of life. We disconnect from our phones and reconnect with nature.

Every campervan holiday, we'd rent a new style of van and one of our favourite campfire conversations would be what we would and wouldn't do if we had a campervan of our

'We've poured so much of ourselves into the build that it really does feel like a home away from home.'

own. Without realising it, we were forming an image of our perfect van which could only be achieved if we built it ourselves. We like to think we are practical folk, but neither of us had any carpentry, mechanical or engineering experience so we knew this would be quite a challenge.

The beauty of building your own van means that it can turn out exactly how you dream it to be: our garage stores all our adventure gear, our large kitchen accommodates our love of cooking, our wood burner reflects our love of campfires and our roof deck allows us to gaze across the places our van takes us to – often with a G&T in our hands. We've poured so much of ourselves into the build that it really does feel like a home away from home. We are so glad we converted it ourselves because not only did we create our dream campervan but we also discovered a new passion for van building.

The Grizzly is our second campervan conversion, so we had a great idea of what we wanted to achieve beforehand. We took all our favourite things about our first van – like our big kitchen, wooden ceiling and comfortable lounging space – and levelled them up. We then added new things that we knew would make it into the ultimate adventure van. We wanted a fixed bed so we wouldn't have to make up and take down the bed every day, and underneath that bed we wanted a big garage space to accommodate the ever-growing gear for all our hobbies and our ever-growing dog, Bear. We wanted a wood-burning stove as we

love nothing more than a campfire and wanted to bring that feeling inside.

Our main focus, which didn't change, was that practicality and storage would always take priority in our design. We wanted our van to fit around our needs and make life on the road as simple and streamlined as possible. When living in a tiny space, even if only for a brief time, simplicity and practicality are key. If there are elements that don't work well then living in the van soon turns into total chaos.

Our approach to the conversion budget was much like our approach to build plans: rather than having a fixed cost and idea in mind, we would start with one thing and let the van evolve. It's not an approach that suits everyone, but it really works for us. This way we didn't get hung up on things if they didn't go to plan – something that happens a lot in van building! We painstakingly researched every product to make sure we got the best item for the best price. We prefer travelling in the winter, so our luxuries are all about keeping warm. That is why we treated ourselves to a hot-water tank, wood burner and gas heater. I really feel the cold, but in our van that is never a problem. It's like a cosy cabin on wheels!

I remember exactly when we first saw a van which didn't look like a classic prefabricated campervan – The Rolling Home on Instagram. When we saw that vans didn't have to look like they were made of plastic, it set our imaginations blazing. I really feel The Rolling Home introduced the idea of 'vanlife' to a lot of us

'Our biggest dream is to ship the van across to Canada and the USA for the ultimate road trip. Hopefully, one day soon!'

and I will be forever grateful to them for doing so. We follow a lot of campervan projects on Instagram and it continues to amaze me how creative people can be. We are forever being inspired by other people's campervans, and we are always adding ideas to our growing checklist of what we can include on our future projects.

It's safe to say that we have developed a Camper Dreamin' style as our builds have evolved. We love how the combination of wood and bold colour can create a really cosy environment, even when it's situated in a rolling metal box. But what's shaped our van the most is our hobbies. Laurie is a keen downhill rider and I'm falling in love mountain biking, so bike storage was essential. Our entire van was built around making sure Laurie's beloved bike could fit underneath the bed! We love to climb as well, and we need places to store all our gear so it doesn't get damp or damaged. We both enjoy stand-up paddleboarding and we needed to make sure there was space to store the boards as well. It was quite a challenge in such a small space, but we made it work. Another unique element of our build is our roof deck; it has a lift-up back so we can lounge up there with a drink and watch the world go by. We often get a lot of bemused looks from passers-by!

Our absolute favourite feature in our van is our wood burner; we call it the heart of our rolling home. To us there is no better way to finish off a day of adventure than sitting around a fire, whether it's a campfire or our wood burner. It does a fantastic job of keeping the van warm at a consistent temperature with minimal effort and creates such a wonderful ambience. Plus, you can brew your cuppa on it!

When we inevitably build our next van (hopefully, many years down the line), we may decide to install an internal shower and toilet. We've been happily relying on public loos and our external shower until now, but with so many public toilets being closed down this is becoming more challenging for us. We've recently invested in a 'portapotty', which we plan to store in our seating. It's not exactly glamorous, but then vanlife often isn't.

One thing that always breaks our hearts is seeing litter in nature and when travelling in a campervan you notice it even more. We've always taken a 'leave it better than we found it' approach to our travelling and try to pick up other people's trash in beauty spots, in the hope of making the next visitor's experience more enjoyable. Unfortunately, a minority of people leaving their rubbish behind is a continuing problem and, understandably, local communities are getting fed up; sometimes they direct their frustrations towards the vanlife community. We really wanted to try to turn this around and so founded The Leave It Better Community, a considerate campervan and camping collective. Whether it's wild spaces, urban park-ups, locals (both human and wild) or the places we pass through, the community's aim is to leave them better than we found them. This involves litter picking,

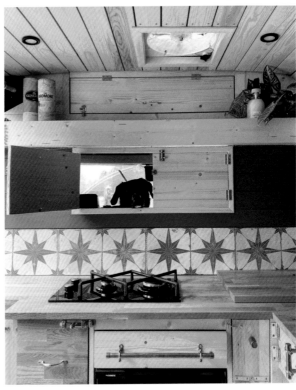

a next level leave-no-trace ethos and making sure we respect the locals and support the communities in any way we can. The response has been incredible, and we hope to continue to spread this positive message to fellow van-lifers and small communities alike.

Our favourite place to escape to in the van is Scotland and we have been making it a yearly pilgrimage since we started vanlife. The combination of stunning scenery, endless mountain ranges and its vast wilderness makes Scotland the best and most beautiful adventure playground. We are wild campers at heart, and in Scotland it is easy to escape from civilisation and lose yourself in the wilderness. We love it so much that one day we hope to make Scotland our home.

Our passion for transforming vans into adventure campervans has inevitably steered us on to a whole new adventure – our new conversion business 'Camper Dreamin' Conversions'. And, of course, there will be many more road trips and van adventures on the horizon; we especially look forward to taking the van across to Europe and spending more time in the Alps. Our biggest dream is to ship the van across to Canada and the USA for the ultimate road trip. Hopefully, one day soon!

Follow Izzy, Laurie and Bear's adventures on Instagram at camperdreamin and www.camperdreamin.com, and learn more about The Leave It Better Community on Instagram at leaveitbetterco.

THE GRIZZLY

Biggest challenge: Storing biking and paddle boarding equipment in a small space
Favourite feature: Wood-burning stove
Favourite destination: The wilderness of Scotland
Camping ethos: Leave a place better than you found it.
Future plans: Continue to lovingly craft campervans so others can fulfil their own camper dreams.

DAVE THE PARCELFORCE TRUCK

Charlie Glover is a vehicle converter based in Cheltenham, Gloucestershire, who lives in his own converted ex-ParcelForce lorry.

The idea of living in a vehicle came to me while I was travelling through the Western Australian Outback in 2011. I'd broken down in my 1982 Toyota Hilux, nicknamed Bumblebee, in the remote town of Carnarvon. By the time I'd fixed the truck I couldn't afford accommodation, so to save money I turned the pick-up area into a basic bedroom and kitchen and thus began my love of living in vehicles.

Jump forward a few years and I found myself driving lorries across England and Europe for an events company. Because I was always on the road, sleeping in the lorry or hotels, I found myself being away more than actually being home. At the time, home was an overpriced , damp, basement room and I hated paying rent for somewhere I was barely seeing. After a while, I'd had enough and the hunt for a suitable vehicle to live in was on.

As an HGV driver, I have a licence to drive any size of vehicle, so I wasn't limited to looking for a small van to turn into my new home. I found my now beautiful – but at the time, very faded and rusty – ex-ParcelForce truck in March 2018 and bought it for the grand total of £2,200.

I've always loved upcycling and making beautiful things from what some would call rubbish, so I decided that instead of a buying new fittings for the truck I would create a much homelier version out of what I could find and salvage. Plus rubbish is usually free so that definitely helped with the cost of the build!

At the start it definitely wasn't comfortable and glamorous by any means. I moved into the truck on day four of the build – the second I had a side door fitted. This was in mid-March, so it was cold and drafty with no heating, no toilet and no shower. But that's what I loved about the process; some nights are awful, but when the sun shines and you remember you're making your own home, it makes it all worthwhile.

I started working on the van in March 2018 and I don't think I will ever say the truck is finished as I'm always upgrading, tweaking or realising that I did something wrong in the first place - which means I have to rip it out and start again. Through the whole process I've made many mistakes, learnt from them, and thoroughly enjoyed it.

The floor is made of scaffold boards and the ceiling is cladding from an old shed that I saved

> *'You have a plan at the beginning but once you start to work on and live in it, everything changes and adapts to what you need.'*

from being burnt. I lightly sanded it and that gave the beautiful finish you can see. I have a basic gas hot-water system for my shower, the water for which comes from some upcycled beer kegs I found in a derelict pub and modified. I also have a gas hob, oven, sink and a Dometic compressor fridge-freezer.

There are two 265W solar panels on the roof which charge up my four 85ah lithium batteries, which give me more than enough juice to run everything I could ever want, including my sound system, which I salvaged from a nightclub whilst travelling in Australia.

All of the kitchen units and drawers used to be part of a university showroom. I saved them from the skip and made doors out of old pallets. The kitchen backsplash is made of slate I found on a friend's farm down in Cornwall.

In one of my skip-diving adventures I came across a roll of fake grass which I attached to my tail lift to create my infinity lawn, which is perfect for sitting on and enjoying a cold beer in the summer. My gran especially loves the way I can lower the tail lift so she can hop on, and I can lift her up inside to admire my handiwork.

As well as the necessities, I've added a couple of creature comforts. I have a sound system installed that I saved from a nightclub I helped to renovate in Australia. I have a super-efficient fridge which runs off lithium batteries, meaning I've always got cold beer.

On the wall are displayed my festival passes from my time working in Australia with a massive print of a photo I took whilst travelling in my old Hilux.

I wouldn't say I've made many mistakes while converting my truck, though designs do change throughout the process. You have a plan at the beginning but once you start to work on and live in it, everything changes and adapts to what you need.

The outside is amazing, as you can see from the pictures. Every September, the Paint Festival in Cheltenham celebrates street art; this is where I'm currently based and I thought the truck might be great blank canvas for one of the artists.

Little did I know that the artist MyDogSighs was more than up for the challenge. He painted the truck over four days in a cold wet carpark and I love the end result. It attracted a lot of admiring looks through the festival and is easily recognised while I'm moving around town.

I've been living full-time in the truck for nearly four years now, and I wouldn't change it for anything. I don't do much travelling in the truck, but that was never my intention. It was all about having my own affordable home that I could come back to after a long week of being away at work. I love the freedom of not having to worry about leaving things like your phone charger at home as no matter where you are, you're home. The view changes, your neighbours change, but you're still home with everything you need.

MYDOGSIGHS

Mydogsighs, the street artist who created Dave's unique exterior: 'Since being a nipper and prizing my Hot Wheels car collections, I have always been disappointed as a grown-up that real vehicles lack the excitement of my childhood toys. When asked to paint the truck for Cheltenham Paint Festival I knew I had an opportunity to bring my childhood dream to life.

Using my trademark eyes and flames reminiscent of a Hot Wheels classic, I set about transforming this exciting home into a touring art piece.'

🅞 mydogsighs

'Knowing I built everything myself, using my own hands to create what I describe as a dream house on wheels, makes it even more meaningful.'

I'd never planned on full-time vanlife due to being away for work and often travelling abroad during the winter, but during the coronavirus pandemic in 2020 my work dried up and meant that I was unable to travel. Since I'm now in the van full-time, a few things have had to change. I upgraded my solar setup on the roof and bought four lithium batteries to go with it so I don't need to charge up as often.

I still don't have any real plan on travelling a long distance or road tripping in the truck, it's just a wonderful way to live life. Knowing I built everything myself, using my own hands to create what I describe as a dream house on wheels, makes it even more meaningful.

I don't have one particular favourite moment in the van, but the first time I was able to use the tail lift to lift my gran so she could see my home was very special. The day the exterior of the van was finished, I hosted the truck's first 'house party'. I was parked in a gravel carpark, disposable BBQs on the go, and my friends were able to come check out my new 'house'. This was the first time anyone had really seen the van up close and in person, which made the whole event all the more memorable.

Since the Covid crisis my life and circumstances have changed, so much so that I've recently set up my own conversion business, RanVanga. Based in Cheltenham, my aim is to create high-end, yet affordable, motorhomes. I've already sold a few vans to extremely happy customers and I'm thoroughly enjoying the chance to create homes for others, long after I moved into my own home on wheels.

◎ Learn more about Charlie's builds on Instagram at ranvanga.

DAVE

Upcycled features:
Kitchen furniture from a university showroom
Backsplash from slate found on a farm
Fake grass for infinity lawn found while skip diving
Freshwater storage in beer kegs rescued from derelict pub
Sound system saved from an out-of-business nightclub
Future plans: Developing my vehicle conversion business, RanVanga, so others can enjoy a home on wheels as well.

ORANGE ROAD TRIP

Lisa and Janek, from Bonn in Germany, met back in high school and have been together for over six years now. Lisa is currently doing her masters in sustainable marketing and Janek is doing an apprenticeship as a refrigerator and air-conditioning engineer.

We always loved to travel together and even before we got our driving licences we went on a few camping trips with a tent together. Then we finally got our driving licences and Lisa got a Volkswagen Caddy, a little van, for her eighteenth birthday. Within three weeks and with a budget of €200 we converted that car into a small camper and started vanlife by exploring the south coast of France. The van only had a bed and a few storage spaces in the back, so travelling in it wasn't very comfortable, but we loved that style of travelling and all the freedom it gives you. We could just stop wherever we wanted and found so many amazing places along our journeys. But the longer we travelled with our Caddy, the more we felt the need for a bigger van and a bit more privacy, especially as we wanted to be able to live like this for longer periods. The Caddy is still with us though and serves us as our everyday car.

After weeks of research, we finally found our van, Carl, which was previously owned by the German civil protection. This meant that it was in a really good shape when we bought it and had a really low mileage. Carl is a 1980 Mercedes 407D with 72 horsepower and needs about 15 litres of diesel per 100km. We mainly chose him because of the reliable motor and technique, but with 510m length and 215m width, it also offered enough space to build in everything that we wanted. With 80km/h average speed, we're not very fast while travelling, but the ride itself has become a part of our journey. We have already spotted the weirdest and coolest things while driving through lonely landscapes.

When we bought the van, it already contained some spartan furnishing, consisting of a bed and a wardrobe. We used this setup for our first trips in order to find out what we really needed and wanted to have in our van. After a couple of months, we started the conversion by pulling out everything in there. Then we insulated everything, wired all the electricity and began building our furniture. Of course, while building our van there were times when things didn't go as planned and when we felt lost and desperate, but as we had a clear goal in mind

'Our van gave us the freedom to choose what we wanted to experience and where we wanted to go every day.'

we were able to motivate each other and realise our dream.

In our van we opted for a fixed bed and a lot of wooden elements to create a cosy atmosphere. Now, the 6m² in the back of our van are filled with a bed, a couch, a kitchen and lots of storage space. We are also able to have a warm shower outside as we built in a water heater that runs on gas. On our roof we mounted two solar panels, which usually fill up our batteries during the day, so we're self-sufficient and don't have to stay at campgrounds. In order to heat up the van on colder days and nights, we also added a small wood stove inside. The conversion of our van into a little home took us about six months, but we couldn't work full-time on the van during that time as we still had to work and take exams. In total we spend about €6,000 on the conversion – that probably sounds like a lot, but we wanted to build something long-lasting, so we mostly opted for high-quality materials, especially regarding electronics. We also changed some things on the exterior of the van. We added bigger rims, which means we can go off-road a bit more, built a new roof rack and added a bigger fuel tank.

When we finally finished our van build we started our biggest journey so far. For three months we explored south-eastern Europe and got to know Bosnia and Herzegovina, Montenegro, Albania and Greece. On this trip, we found that travelling in a van gives you the opportunity to really slow down and experience a country and its culture in a totally different way from other travellers. Especially in the Balkans, we were warmly welcomed and quite surprised about the hospitality and openness of the locals. We had the chance to explore the most beautiful landscapes, while our van gave us the freedom to choose what we wanted to experience and where we wanted to go every day. If we liked somewhere, we could stay there as long as we wanted and if we didn't like a place, we would just get into the van and drive to somewhere new.

In all the places we have visited so far – which is most of southern Europe – the people were quite interested in who we are and what we do, so it was pretty easy to learn about the country's culture and the people who lived there. We really enjoy being surrounded by people, but while travelling you also need time to relax in order to process the things you have experienced. Living in a van means that you can choose where to stay, so we had the opportunity to spend a few days in nature and quietness whenever we felt overwhelmed, and that's one of the things we love the most about travelling in a van.

What actually surprised us the most about life on the road was how little you actually need to live. At home, we have tons of stuff we rarely use – or don't use at all. Since we don't have a lot of space in our van, we had to pick out the things we really needed and wanted to have with us. We learned that we don't need as much stuff as we thought in order to be happy.

'People help whenever and wherever they can!'

The other thing that surprised us is how helpful people you don't know can be when you're in need. People help whenever and wherever they can!

Last year we spent a month in Portugal and wanted to explore more of Europe with our van but, as we all know, life had different plans and instead we all ended up in lockdown. So we were looking for new projects and came across a van that we couldn't resist buying. He's almost the same model as our van, Carl, but has a bigger engine and used to be a furniture transporter, so there's a huge box on it (5m² x 30m). This gives us the chance to build a whole new home on wheels. The main reason for buying this new van is that we really missed the standing height in our first van and we couldn't travel with our van in winter as it's not very well insulated. For now, we'll keep both vans, as we love our small one too much and it will probably take a lot of time to convert the big truck. Until then, we'll continue to explore the world, seeing its beauty and all its unique features by driving along its roads with Carl, while experiencing the freedom we love in our lives!

⊙ Follow Lisa and Janek's adventures on Instagram at orangeroadtrip.

CARL

Main attraction:	Reliable motor and plenty of space
Cost of conversion:	€6,000
Ethos:	You don't need as much as stuff as you think to be happy.
Favourite part of vanlife:	Ability to spend time in quiet nature when overwhelmed.
Future plans:	Converting our new truck while continuing to travel in Carl.

THE HENDERSONS

Lauren and Robin own The Hendersons, an online lifestyle shop. In 2018 they converted a van to go on a nine-month trip around Europe, starting in the Arctic Circle and travelling to twenty-seven countries.

We have always had a desire to travel, and we loved the thought of living in a little mobile home we had created. The idea of driving along the winding roads of the Black Forest or through the hill-top villages of Tuscany appealed to us. We had been on many single destination holidays and this really seemed like a change. Living in a van persuades you to encounter things you wouldn't on a city break or a cottage holiday – not to mention the people you meet or the problems you have to overcome on the road.

After catching the travelling bug, our can-do attitude along with our small budget made converting the van ourselves the only option we wanted to pursue. We were lucky enough to use our parents' drive as a base for the work; there were many trips to the DIY store and a whole lot of mistakes, but the satisfaction you feel when you drive around in a little home on wheels you created yourself is unbeatable!

Although we were eager to get the ball rolling initially, there was a whole lot we had to learn – from the correct type of insulation to how to fit and wire-up solar panels. We had to learn it all. We weren't too harsh on ourselves as everything was a learning curve and none of the issues along the way made us re-think our decision. YouTube videos were great if we didn't know how to do something as there are tutorials for everything online; as long as you're confident, you can do most things on a self-build!

We were still working full-time whilst converting the van. We knew it had to be comfortable, as most of our time would be spent either driving the van or sitting in the back, especially in the first few months when we decided to head up to the Arctic Circle for winter. We also knew it had to be robust – driving thousands of miles around Europe we didn't want any malfunctions or disasters. We kept things simple and the benefit of installing everything yourself, is that if things do go wrong, you know how to fix it. Our biggest luxury and most expensive item on the build was the fridge; because we had to conserve gas we bought a domestic fridge which runs on a tiny amount of 12V electricity and also has a freezer. Because of this fantastic little fridge, we

'When living in a van, you learn to make the most of the little things.'

were able to enjoy cold beers in the 35-degree heat in the south of France! Our biggest bargain was our vintage gas stove, which we bought off a lady whose father bought the stove back in the seventies for a campervan project but never used it! It was pristine, in its original box and had all its original paperwork, and we got it for the grand total of £30! Our budget for the whole project was around £3,000–£4,000, not including the actual van. We saved when we could, but spent the money on things that we would heavily rely on.

Our desire to travel has always been apparent. We were lucky enough to be in a position in our lives where we didn't have any huge commitments and were free to make the leap into a big adventure – so we did, and it's the best thing we have ever done.

As we run our own little business (a vintage boutique) from our van, we knew it had to be comfortable not only to live in but also work in. We had to allocate space for vintage finds along the way, and because we were passionate about vintage, we often visited salvage yards during our build, which is a top tip – that and boot fairs! We managed to find a perfect little Belfast sink which we fitted in the van; although it weighs a ton it was so cute we couldn't help but incorporate it into the van!

On one occasion, we screwed through the locking mechanism on the rear door of the van, which prevented the rear door locking. After a huge amount of investigation and ripping half the back end of the van out, we finally discovered the fault – the smallest screw that was

slightly stopping the mechanism from closing. But it's from these mistakes that you learn and find out more about the workings of your van!

One thing we are proud of is the van layout and how we managed to fit the huge amount of storage space in the van for everything we needed for a whole year! We also enjoyed using reclaimed materials and seeing how we could incorporate them into the van, such as a 1960s kitchen cupboard which we used as storage space under our bed. It would have taken twice as long to make something like that from scratch and it is very light, which is another thing you have to consider when building a van. Both our driving licences only allowed us to drive vehicles up to 3.5 tons and when we were all loaded up we were slightly under that, so it's definitely something to bear in mind.

When building a van, you have to think very carefully about your aims and what you wish to achieve whilst living in it. Because we were planning on heading to the Arctic in January, we had to think carefully about the practicalities and things that would be necessary for such an extreme trip. For heating, we had to decide whether to fit a log burner or a diesel heater. Our budget wouldn't cover both, but as we're both massive fans of real log burners we thought it would be the most homely feature in the van. We have also cooked on it, which helped conserve the limited amount of gas we could fit in the van. If we were to do the trip again, we would like to get a diesel heater as well as the log burner, just for ease and efficiency. If you are fitting a log burner, be sure

'We gained friends who we will always remember.'

to check all the regulations and you must have a carbon monoxide alarm fitted in the van; we had two just in case. Throughout the whole trip, it only went off once – when we burnt some toast under the grill!

Our trip took us to all corners of Europe, experiencing some of the worst snowfall Norway had seen in thirty years (1 metre in twenty-four hours!) to learning how to manage reindeer, and experiencing a free music festival in the Italian hills. When living in a van, you learn to make the most of the little things: opening your van door and seeing a secluded beach in Croatia, hearing owls during the night whilst in the wilds of the Black Forest. There were a whole load of 'firsts' for us whilst in the van: the first time driving a tractor, the first time we experienced temperatures as low as -40°C, the first time we drove snowmobiles – not to mention all the culinary firsts along the way! It would be hard to pick a single defining memory, though sitting around the campfire in the beautiful Slovenian countryside with great company, but with no commitments, no bills to pay and no time limit on how long we could stay was probably the most liberated we have ever felt.

Our trip took us to twenty-seven countries; each one was beautifully unique and we have memories from them all that we will treasure forever. Sweden will always feel like a second home to us. We first visited Sweden a couple of years before our vanlife adventure started and we couldn't wait to go back. Something about the endless forests, the huge open lakes and the wilderness appeals to us. Whilst travelling, we were taken aback by the sheer beauty of Switzerland. The hillside lodges, the beautiful tiny cable cars taking people up and down the mountains, along with the snow-covered peaks – there aren't many places like it. The Lofoten Archipelago in Norway was also pretty special with its tiny fishing villages; the famous Henningsvaer football pitch was a must-see for us and it didn't disappoint.

One thing which made our vanlife adventure even better was the people we met on the way, from forest workers in Poland who welcomed us into their house to for pizza and wine, to other vanlifers doing their thing. We also used the volunteering platform Workaway, through which we stayed with four families during our trip, including Sami reindeer herders in the Arctic and a fantastic family in the southern hills of Slovenia. After a couple of weeks with each family, we gained friends who we will always remember.

Since returning from our nine-month European adventure we have had to commit ourselves to our business for the time being. But a new van will be on the horizon very soon and our need for adventure has been fuelled even more by the incredible time we had in our van.

Follow Lauren and Robin's adventures and learn more about their shop on Instagram at thehendersonsshop and at their website thehendersonsshop.co.uk.

THE HENDERSONS

Biggest luxury: Fridge (worth it for the cold beers!)

Best bargain: Our vintage stove for only £30!

Biggest oops moment: Screwing through the locking mechanism!

First experiences with the van:

     First time driving a tractor

     First time experiencing -40°C

     First time driving snowmobiles

Most defining memory: Sitting around a campfire in the Slovenian countryside.

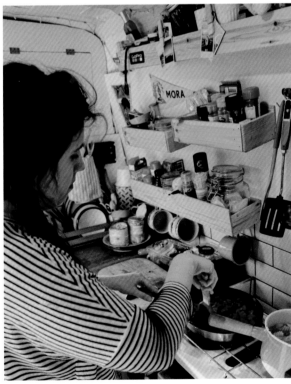

FLORENCE THE AMBULANCE

Mark and Sophie's journey together began at the end of 2018. Their second date was on Christmas Eve in Mark's VW T4, Betsy. He had transformed Betsy into a miniature grotto filled with furry blankets, fairy lights and Christmas-scented candles. Sophie knew then he was a keeper!

When we first met, Mark was staying in his converted campervan part-time and he used it for days out and holidays with his three children. Having a little home on wheels really helped our relationship to flourish in the beginning. I (Sophie) had two small children from a previous marriage; finding the time to date was scarce. My amazing mum helped out a lot and Mark would pull up and make us both dinner in his van. I could relax, knowing I wasn't far away should Mum call me back.

There was only one slight issue: when cooking all these delicious meals, the van was too small for Mark to stand while he cooked. That was when we decided a bigger van was needed. Food and cooking are things we are both passionate about and we knew cooking in the van would become a regular activity. Therefore, we needed a bigger space.

In April 2019, Mark mentioned the idea of buying an ex-ambulance but I wasn't keen! Having worked in the NHS as a radiographer since 2008, I had seen my fair share of gore and gruesomeness. Cooking and sleeping in a place that had potentially seen every bodily fluid known, as well as people possibly passing away, was not very appealing. Mark was adamant it was perfect; they are spacious, already have electrics in the back, and are usually regularly serviced with genuine parts used for any replacements. I still wasn't convinced.

In May 2019, I received a phone call from Mark informing me that he had just purchased an ex-ambulance and it would be arriving the following week. When it arrived, it looked exactly like an ambulance! Minus the blue lights and sirens, the AMBULANCE letters, although removed, were clearly visible where the yellow paint had faded around them. The inside was an actual treasure trove, everything was still in place: the stretcher, fold-away seat – even the cupboards with labels indicating what had previously lived in each one. My personal favourites were the cupboards labelled 'vomit bowl' and 'body bag'. Seeing the inside up-close was when my love for the idea began. Just like Mark, I adored that this vehicle had such an interesting history. Mark saw it as giving 'her' a new lease of life in her retirement.

We are regularly asked whether the van is haunted or told how disgusting it is because of the nature of what happens in the back of an ambulance. But we prefer to see the positive side of it and remind people of the number of individuals our ambulance has helped to save, racing along streets, lights flashing, sirens blaring to save the person in the back. Not to mention the amazing paramedics working tirelessly day after day in there. Two of the paramedics who worked in Florence saw her online and reached out to us on Instagram. The fact that they remembered that particular ambulance and shared some memories made the conversion even more special to us.

After thinking about all of this, there was only one name suitable for our mobile home – Florence, after Florence Nightingale, of course! In answer to the many times we've been asked, there are no ghosts in our ambulance – that we've seen anyway!

On to the conversion! Mark had skilfully converted his first van from a traditional mini-bus-style van to a cosy campervan, and this one was going to be no different. Mark's profession is based in IT, but he has always enjoyed building things and so decided to take on the conversion single-handedly. The ambulance cost £5,000 and we allowed a budget of £2,000

for the conversion. This was another reason Mark decided to complete the renovation without any help: to help keep the costs low.

He set about ripping all the ambulance innards from the back. This was no easy task – everything in the back of an ambulance is VERY secure! Not only were the cupboards glued in place there were screws for extra security. It was quite the undertaking. Once bare, Florence was given a very thorough clean, including all the nooks and crannies to ensure she was up to scratch.

One of the great things about buying an ambulance is it is already insulated to a certain degree. We set about insulating it further, and adding our chosen flooring. The original layout we decided on included a fixed double bed at the rear of the van, a small shower room with a toilet, a kitchen area and a seating area. We wanted to keep some of the character of Florence and decided to keep some of the original units. Another great thing about buying a used ambulance is that there is lots of storage available, and everything has lockable doors. A definite positive for a lived-in van!

To try to limit the cost of the conversion, we decided to use as many upcycled, recycled and reclaimed items as possible. We felt this was a great way to give items a new lease of life and prevent them ending up in a landfill. As already mentioned, we decided to keep some items from the ambulance and reuse them in the build. Facebook marketplace and car boot

sales became our new best friends. The bed was built using slats from Mark's children's old bunk beds, the kitchen unit was rescued after being thrown away. The sink, foldaway table and curtains were bargains from Facebook marketplace. Mark received quite a few funny glances when he was parked up by the river, doors open with the sewing machine whirring away whilst he adjusted the curtains.

We found a lot of bargains in the van build due to using so many upcycled items. The biggest luxury in the van is most likely the TV (which was free!) or when Mark sometimes takes his PlayStation on trips with him. An unexpected bargain was the mattress for the bed, which cost just £70 and ended up being the most comfortable mattress either of us have ever slept on.

The conversion took two months; we spent the evenings together painting and decorating the inside, but the majority of the hard work fell to Mark. He watched videos on YouTube for ideas and inspiration for a particular part of the build. Within a couple of hours, he would have worked out how to do it and built it. A prime example of this was a pull-out bench seat which took the place of the shower room. We made this change to ensure there was enough space for everyone to sleep on family trips.

Over the summer, we had many lovely date nights in the van, adventures with just the two of us, and with the children. But not all together – that would definitely have been a squeeze! The highlights of these include trips to Dorset and parking up on the Isle of Portland, as well as a trip in the Surrey hills for Mark and his children. Towards the end of 2019, Mark was looking at the V5 and realised that Florence was a little bigger than they had once thought, and was actually over the weight limit for their standard driving licences – oops! This meant Florence had to spend a little time off the road whilst Mark completed a C1 driving test, including theory and practical. We spent evenings in the van practising the theory questions. Mark had never imagined he would have to worry about learning about electrical lines to trailers and even moving livestock!

At this point, Mark was in the van pretty much full-time and began cooking more and more in there. This was also when Covid hit, and everyone was plunged into lockdown. We decided to use this time constructively to do two things: firstly, create Vanlife Eats! This is an online community for people to share their favourite things to make and eat in their vans with fellow vanlifers. There are also several informative articles and product reviews relating to campervan kitchens and cooking in tiny spaces.

The second thing was to renovate Florence once more. As our van cooking began to take off and we were taking more photos and filming videos in the van, we realised a bigger kitchen was needed. With Mark being in the van almost full-time now, the decision was

made to put the shower room back in. The van looks much more spacious now without the fixed bed, and it is easy to convert the seating area to a bed within five minutes. Although the super comfy mattress is missed, this configuration gives the best use of space, particularly for family days out. It provides a base to come back to for meals, to warm up, and get changed – plus a toilet!

Florence's exterior also got a make-over so no more being mistaken for an ambulance on the road. When trying to change the vehicle class (benefits include cheaper insurance, plus an ambulance is tax exempt!), we were turned down because Florence still looked like the ambulance she once was. Therefore, with a heavy heart, we decided to paint her. We painted her ourselves using paint designed for army vehicles, and with the help of Mark's oldest children. No longer will other road users be giving us priority – a definite bonus of having an ex-ambulance.

So, what is next for Florence and us? Vanlife Eats is growing every day so expect lots more cooking, a van tour on YouTube and certainly many more adventures. We are also planning many UK trips with the children and romantic breaks for just the two of us, as well as hoping to attend lots of campervan festivals. One place both of us would love to visit in Florence is Scotland, having seen so many amazing photos from fellow vanlifers, and so that definitely makes our list of future places to go, in particular the North Coast 500 route.

Converting an ex-ambulance was such a fun and rewarding experience, and now she is a much-loved part of our family. It hasn't always been plain sailing though and we encountered a number of setbacks along the way.

Follow Mark, Sophie and Florence's adventures on Instagram at florencetheambulance. Vanlife Eats is a community for people to share their favourite things to make and eat in their vans with fellow vanlifers; follow @vanlife_eats for more information.

FLORENCE

Converting an Ex-Ambulance Tips:

- Ambulance electrics are complicated! They are powered through a system unique to ambulances and it can be very tricky to work out. Do your research, and ask for advice in ambulance conversion groups. The kind people in these groups have helped us so much. Sometimes you may need to refer to an expert, particularly if you are not overly familiar with electrics.
- Think about the class category you want your van to be. Ambulances are tax exempt, so you may need to change it to a van with side windows while completing your conversion in order to tax it or declare it SORN. If travelling on ferries etc., you may need to book as a campervan due to having gas in the vehicle; this may still be possible without it being classed as a campervan legally, but it may be something to consider.
- Look at the gross weight of the vehicle! Many ambulances have upgraded suspension systems so that if CPR is taking place in the back the van is stabilised. It's a great feature; it means we rarely have to worry about being parked on a slant as it auto adjusts. The system is super heavy though. This means that if you are not planning on removing this or the lift at the back, then the weight after the conversion could mean you require a specialist licence.

Extra tip: Want curtains in your van but can't fit a curtain pole? Sew magnets into the hem of the curtains so they can fasten to the van, without any need for poles!

RECYCLE INN

Yasmine El Kotni and René Brink are vanlifers with a focus on upcycling and being environmentally friendly. Based in France, they have just started their van conversion business after the success of their own conversion.

The main reason we converted our first vehicle was our love of travelling. René is from Australia, so he was very used to the culture of travelling around in a van even though he'd never done it before we converted ours. I (Yasmine) am from France and this was all completely new to me! When we arrived in New Zealand, aiming to stay for a year, we wanted to explore the remote parts of it without being part of mass tourism. For us, living in a van was the only way to travel slowly, without rushing and having to look for hostels every other night so we could really soak in the magnificent views that Aotearoa has to offer.

Back in France, we knew we would want a van for the same reason: going off the beaten tracks and exploring areas that you wouldn't discover if you didn't take the chance to get lost. Our favourite places always end up to be the ones we discovered by accident.

When I arrived alone in New Zealand, I was on a budget and had no space to build the van, so I decided to get a van already semi-converted. It was a family bubble car with a plank of wood and a proper mattress on top

of it – when I laid down, I was so close to the ceiling it felt like being in a cage. At the back, there was another plank to use as a benchtop. When René joined me, it was far too cramped for two people. Over five days we pulled some pallets apart, made a low sliding bed, a little folding table and built a way more functional kitchen at the back. It felt more homely straight away.

Knowing that we would stay longer, we decided to convert a bigger van. By then we had an outdoor space to work in and had discovered the amazing op shops of New Zealand. We built our first 'real size' van, Woody, in about two weeks and lived in it on the road for a few months.

For our most recent conversion here in France, we were really nervous because there are a lot of regulations here when it comes to van building. But we finally wrapped our heads around them pretty quickly and had the chance to build it at a friend's place, and he had so many old interesting things floating around we managed to build the van of our dreams – mainly out of repurposed materials.

'Working with upcycled materials can be quite a brain teaser.'

Before the conversion, we had trouble working out the layout we wanted. It was a huge upgrade compared to the previous one as we were going from a L1h1 to a L3h2. We almost had too much space available and weren't used to thinking that big. The regulations also had to be studied so we followed the rules for building campers in France.

The main challenge during the conversion was to make all the reclaimed appliances fit together somehow. When you buy things and appliances brand new you can buy everything to size, but when you reclaim them you usually struggle to make things fit – but what a feeling when you find a perfect match!

We didn't really keep track of the spending budget for our van, but it was quite low as we reclaimed most of the materials and we took our time during the build. The biggest bargain was our little oven which cost only €50 – the brand-new ones are so expensive these days! We actually don't have anything very expensive in the van. The priciest item is the wastewater tank that we had to buy brand new so the dimensions fit under the car, and we only paid €90 for it.

We both are big fans of treehouses and we love the builds of Nelson Treehouse. Taking inspiration from those impressive cabins in trees, we decided to add some branches in our builds and get that cosy cabin feel.

Converting this van from scratch meant we could decide on all aspects of the build. René is a muralist and visual artist (@_rene_brink_/renebrink.com) and I often work on the laptop so we decided to build a desk at a comfortable height and looking out of the window.

I created an environmental non-for-profit organisation in France that raises awareness on small single-use plastic objects like straws (@baslespailles/baslespailles.org) and led to their ban in January 2021. Our environmental impact is very important to both of us and it is mainly why we decided to use reclaimed material instead of buying brand new items.

We both are big plant lovers, so we dedicated a lot of space to plants. We have a cabinet at the entrance of the van created from a recycled window to display them; it's like a little greenhouse as well. We also have a dipping tray behind the benchtop that is tiled and sealed inside and allows us to soak the plants if it's really hot or if we are leaving the van for a while.

Cooking is another big passion for us so we dedicated a big chunk of the space to the kitchen and built a large benchtop.

The build went well in general, but we didn't really have a sheltered workspace at the time and converted the van in the middle of winter so the task included many short days and a lot of rain. It was frustrating at times when we couldn't make big progress because of the weather.

Working with upcycled materials can be quite a brain teaser when it comes to fixtures; neither of us really likes plumbing and working on the water and gas was the least enjoyable part of the build as no second-hand items had the same size of fixtures.

When we first went camping in our bubble car we hadn't put curtains in yet, so we decided to install them right then and there on the

'What a treat to bake fresh bread while out on the road!'

beach. We had installed all the hooks around except for the very last one … and then we heard a loud fizzing noise. We looked at each other in shock and then a ploom of vapor came flying out. After it dispersed, we realised we had just drilled a hole into the tiniest 6mm air-conditioning pipe and couldn't stop laughing! Luckily, New Zealand never gets too hot! It taught us a valuable lesson for our future builds: always check what's behind the wall before you start drilling.

Our plants are definitely our favourite addition to the van, along with the oven. What a treat to bake fresh bread while out on the road! We are thinking of adding a little petrol heater in the future, not only for comfort but also to reduce the build-up of moisture.

We have fallen in love with so many places during our travels. We both loved the coast of Portugal, and the lakes and mountains around the South Island of New Zealand. It's hard to beat those views!

We love building vans so much that we created our own bespoke van conversion company called Recycle Inn. We had to slow down our travels because of Covid restrictions so we decided to find a place with a big workshop and garden where we could experiment around permaculture. By the end of 2021 we will have already built ten vans, and have another few building projects lined up in the next few months. We really want people to enjoy the ultimate freedom of living in a van as much as we do!

Follow Yasmine and René's adventures on Instagram at recycleinn, see René's art at _rene_brink_ and learn more about single-use plastic objects at baslespailles.org.

RECYCLE INN

Biggest challenge:	Fitting together reclaimed appliances
Best bargain:	Our oven for only €50
Favourite feature:	Our plants
Biggest oops moment:	Drilling into the air-conditioning pipe
Favourite places:	Coast of Portugal and the South Island of New Zealand
Future plans:	Developing our bespoke van conversion company.

BETTY BLUE

Former Labour Party Parliamentary Candidate, RAF veteran, writer, speaker, broadcaster, photographer, self-harm and suicide survivor ... and transgender. Sophie was recently announced as the winner of the Outstanding Contribution to LGBT+ Life Award at the 2020 British LGBT Awards and named as the Thirteenth Most Influential Person in Brighton according to the Brighton Power 100. Here she talks about her experiences living in her horsebox, Betty Blue.

I close my eyes and breathe, the air clean and crisp.

With each exhalation I can feel the stress and negativity leave my body.

It seems like I've been fighting forever, innumerable foes threatening to destroy me. Depression, self-harm, suicide, gender identity and loneliness, the internal battles ready to take up arms whenever the external enemies – prejudice, bigotry, financial concerns and failed relationships – withdraw from prominence.

My hands thrust further into my pockets, searching for warmth, as my breath pours out of my mouth in a plume of steam. Opening my eyes, I gaze heavenward, taking in the infinite cosmos as I bask in the glow of the full moon, bright as day, that casts long, defined shadows on the frozen ground. A bright light appears on the western horizon, rising rapidly to its zenith 220 miles above me and then streaking towards the east at 17,000 miles per hour as it disappears from view. I look at my watch and smile; the International Space Station keeps exceptional time, I think, as I climb the steps into my home.

Home, for me, is freedom.

Freedom from all those battles that I had waged for so long – not least of which was the financial burdens of the modern housing market.

It's the peace and quiet that I need to repair my mental health and to write about the experience. It's the opportunity to explore and discover the world around me, whether it's coming face-to-face with a roe deer as dawn's first light breaks through the mist or gazing back through time at the stars. It's going on adventures with my son.

Home is also a 7.5-ton horsebox called Betty Blue.

When I first decided to give up the lease on my dream home, a beautiful two-bedroom flat with sea views on the Sussex coast, to move into a 30-year-old lorry, I was greeted with one of two reactions. Some showed deep concern, earnestly reassuring me that if I could save some

'I swam in the sea and celebrated my new, albeit crowded, home.'

money then I would soon be able to get another, possibly smaller, flat. Others looked at me with a sense of wonder and jealous awe, exclaiming that I was, literally, living the dream.

I had indeed dreamt of living in a camper for years, but this was a decision born out of necessity rather than romance. I'd been struggling to pay my rent for months and then the coronavirus pandemic caused the cessation of all gatherings, meaning my career as a motivational speaker and stand-up comedian was put on immediate and indefinite hold. Faced with the very real threat of eviction and the possibility of sleeping in my car, I had to get creative.

Looking through the ads on eBay, I perused vehicle after vehicle, ruling them out for not being big enough, not having a permanent bed, not having somewhere to put my motorbike or simply being out of my price range.

Cliff Richard and the Shadows had sold me on the romantic idea of living in a double-decker bus, but the practicalities of where to park, where to drive and the class of driving licence I would need counted against this, despite the bargain basement prices.

Then I saw her; if not love at first sight it was certainly infatuation. A 1989 Ford Cargo Horsebox for £2,500. She already contained a kitchen, shower and space for a double bed above the cab, as well as bench seating that converted to a second double bed. A stable for three horses meant room for my motorbike – even if it did come with hay and some souvenirs of its previous occupants!

On the day that I moved out of my two-bedroom flat, both my storage unit and the truck were full to the ceiling. That first night, I had to rearrange my possessions simply to make a space big enough for me to sleep, but before I went to bed I swam in the sea and celebrated my new, albeit crowded, home.

Over the coming months, little by little, I began to piece together what I needed in order to live comfortably in this veteran truck. The first job was mucking out the area that would eventually become my bedroom.

A special motorbike mounting system from the States allowed me to park my Harley-Davidson in the stables and a full-size double bed was added above the bike, hinged in the middle to raise like a drawbridge and allow loading.

A Popaloo toilet and lid double as a step to gain access to the raised bed and my clothes hang from the racks that once held hay for the horses – as an estate agent would say, 'it's an original feature'. Insulation has been added, but as this is a work in progress it's not completed, and a diesel heater occupies one of the external lockers.

In the lounge area, the bench seating has been replaced with a sofa bed for both comfort and ease of conversion between roles. Storage is always a challenge when living in a small home, whether it has wheels or not, and the double bed above the cab that no one could get into has been repurposed for storing bedding and all manner of items that accompany me on life's journey.

A vintage walnut record cabinet houses part of my 500-LP strong record collection and a

USB-powered turntable keeps me entertained on the road. My guitars adorn the walls of the lounge where pride of place is afforded to my grandfather's table, relieved of its legs and mounted atop a quick release pillar.

Up front, the original Betty Blue, a hula dancing figure that my son and I bought on our last trip away before the pandemic, watches over us. We have a saying that if Betty is dancing then we know it's going to be a good day.

This is not a build that could have featured in an episode of a TV show; it was not planned, budgeted and meticulously executed. This is a home born out of necessity and designed organically while living on the road. Electrical systems have been repaired and improved, solutions have been tried, rejected and replaced. Betty Blue is still a 30-year-old horsebox and most of the post-purchase expenses have fallen into the 'keep her running' category. Furniture has been repurposed, reclaimed and recycled; everything is done on a shoestring. She's a work in progress and what you see today may not be here tomorrow. There are projects in planning, and I will implement them as budget and necessity dictate, but for now she is my beautiful and comfortable home.

In a world where people are so protective of their territory, I love to roam. For me, vanlife is not about being stealthy, living under the radar on a residential street or industrial estate, constantly in fear of a knock on the door or an abusive note on the windscreen. I'm happiest parked up in the countryside, atop the South Downs with nought but cattle and birds for company.

A year into life on the road, we recently celebrated our first anniversary with a new clutch, and I still think that it's the best decision that I have ever made. I've met wonderful characters, visited beautiful locations and made a lot of great memories with my son.

One day soon I hope to cross the sea and travel – don't ask me where because I don't know yet, that's for the road to decide.

Just me, you and Betty Blue.

Follow Sophie's adventures on Instagram at sophiecooktalks and read more about her experiences and career at www.sophiecook.me.uk.

BETTY BLUE

Sophie is an in-demand public speaker, delivering keynote talks internationally, including a TEDx Talk on change, fear, vulnerability, diversity, and mental health. Sophie's autobiography *Not Today: How I Chose Life*, which charts her personal journey from despair to redemption and acts as a self-help book for anyone struggling with their mental health and identity, is out now. She is currently writing her second book and has branched out into acting.

THE ROAD IS OUR HOME

Rob and Emily became fed up with the repetitive 9 to 5 daily grind – working six days a week just to go on holiday once a year felt like a bum deal. They wanted something more fulfilling and enjoyable, so they came up with a game plan: convert a van into a home that they could live, work and travel in.

There were two main deciding factors that brought us to living in a converted van: travel and debt. We were working long hours in unfulfilling jobs, struggling to pay rent and the thought of travel was nothing but a dream; a common yet unfortunate position that so many of us find ourselves in. But that's life isn't it?

Cuddled up on the sofa one evening, we came across a video of a young chap who had travelled the world without a penny to his name. He had thumbed lifts, couch-surfed and backpacked his way around the entire globe. He worked in temporary jobs along the way, living the simple life but really experiencing everything our wonderful planet has to offer. This was a turning point for us; it was the inspiration we needed to look at things a little differently and really take control of our future.

The idea of converting a van didn't come to us at first, but when it did, it made perfect sense. It would give us the freedom to travel in comfort, the chance to take any opportunities that came our way and the ability to pay off the huge debts that had haunted us for so long. We were excited and felt in control of our lives again.

We knew from the start that we wanted to build our own home. We visited conventions, read reviews and looked at myriad different pre-made motorhomes, but none of them excited us. They all looked a bit lifeless and didn't tick all of the boxes for our requirements. Add to that the sheer excitement and satisfaction of planning and converting our own home-on-wheels, it seemed like the obvious choice!

The solution of living in a vehicle came to us fairly organically, but once that seed was planted, we both became addicted to finding others who had done something similar.

Although the 'vanlife' hashtag wasn't in full swing just yet, there were a few YouTube creators who were ahead of the game, such as Nate Murphy and VanDogTraveller, and they provided us with lots of useful information and tips for planning and building.

'A home has to be warm, cosy and comfortable, and our van is exactly that!'

At the time, there wasn't a great deal of information available about converting a van, so researching things such as legal requirements or which materials to use took us a long time and a lot of trial and error.

Before we even bought the van, we had to decide what we needed, what we wanted, and what would be a luxury in the interior design. For example, I had explicitly told Rob that if we were living in the van full-time, a toilet was must! We also both decided we would prefer a solid bed (rather than a fold-up one), and that we needed some garage space for hobby equipment and tools. These requirements set the structure of our layout, and after that it was simply a case of seeing what would fit in the van and what would make our life most comfortable. We are constantly tinkering with the layout of the van as we figure out what works where and what we use/don't use. For example, last year we changed our seating and table area because it just wasn't comfortable enough to use for long periods of time, and we have moved the fridge three times now to make it easier to use and to stop it overheating! There is a lot of trial and error, but finding solutions to little problems like these is incredibly satisfying.

We knew we would be living in the van for many years and wanted to make sure we made our home as comfortable and durable as possible. This was tricky as we were already in debt and had no spare income. Our only option was to move out of our house and sell almost everything we owned to fund the project. Throughout the year and a half it took to complete the conversion, we stayed with various friends and family and continued to work full-time. We worked on the van every evening for eighteen months solid. Emily even managed to complete her master's degree whilst living this way, and once the basics (like toilet, shower and fridge) were installed, we were ready to move into our new home.

Our most expensive luxury was definitely our off-grid power setup. After weeks of research and reading, we took a risk and purchased a pair of lithium LifePo4 batteries; the lithium technology was fairly new to motorhomes and van conversions at the time. It was a very expensive gamble but it paid off and now, years later, lithium is slowly becoming the industry standard.

It wasn't all expensive purchases though; some things in the van cost us nothing, such as the mirror we made from driftwood we found in North Devon or the double bed that we upcycled out of a set of bunk beds.

One of the important things for us when converting the van was that we didn't want to compromise on comfort – if we were going to do this full-time for a long time, then we needed certain luxuries, such as a proper full-size mattress, a toilet, comfortable seating, heating and for things to be as easily accessible as possible. For me, a home has to be warm, cosy and comfortable, and our van is exactly that!

'They are all just as unique and individual as the people that build and live in them.'

We also have a lot of storage for the multitude of hobbies we have, and we've modified the storage solutions over the years to reflect changes in how or where we're living at the time. Our shower/wet room doubles up as somewhere to store wetsuits or raincoats, boards and bikes, and tools fit underneath the bed in the garage area, plus storage for musical instruments and crafty things.

Our van is full of little unique features, but our favourite is most probably the full-size double bed. There's something truly magical about being parked at the beach, listening to waves crash, as we fall asleep on a luxury memory foam mattress. It's a simple, but luxurious, pleasure.

We also have lots of quirky little touches around the van which we love, like the display for the hand-whittled Harry Potter wand Rob made me.

For us, one of the biggest attractions to converting your own vehicle is that they are all just as unique and individual as the people that build and live in them.

From the carpentry to the electrics and gas, to repainting the exterior and mechanical work, we've self-built/made/fabricated/fixed every part of our van ourselves. There's true satisfaction and reassurance that comes from being able to do it yourself.

I can't say that there have been any noticeable mistakes during the conversion, but our setup has changed quite a lot since we first converted the van. As time goes by, our requirements change, our hobbies change, our jobs change and we adapt the layout to reflect this, like the addition of our furry little four-legged friend, Nacho, or the fact that we both work full-time from the van. As our lives change, our home changes right along with us.

We've survived without hot water for all these years, but a hot-water boiler is definitely something we are planning to add in the future – there's no hurry though, the kettle still works!

We have visited so many incredible locations that it would be difficult to list our favourites. But we are true lovers of the coast and if we had to choose only one place to park up, it would be Woolacombe, North Devon. It's a place we both regularly visited before we met and a place we've visited countless times since being together – we even got engaged there. It will always have a place close to our hearts.

We've wanted to take the van to Europe for a while now. Our original plan was to go there in 2019, but unfortunately Rob was diagnosed with cancer that year, and then in 2020 the coronavirus pandemic threw another spanner in the works. We're in no rush though. Rob is making an incredible recovery and we've had the chance to explore the vast majority of the UK, so it's all good.

Since moving into the van, it kind of feels like we've been on a permanent adventure. We've met some of the most incredible people, stayed at the most beautiful locations and created the best memories. Each day presents us with new challenges and opportunities. Living this way has shaped who we are, taught us to live in the moment, do what makes us happy and, most importantly, to embrace change.

It's been an amazing journey so far and we have no intentions of stopping any time soon!

⊙ Follow Rob and Emily's adventures on Instagram at theroadisourhome and at their website www.theroadisourhome.com.

THE ROAD IS OUR HOME

Biggest outlay: Off-grid power setup
Best bargain: Mirror made of driftwood
Favourite feature: Double bed – a simple luxurious pleasure
Essential feature: A toilet!
Future upgrade: Hot-water boiler
Favourite place: Woolacombe, North Devon (if we *had* to choose).
                   It will always have a place close to our hearts.

FIRETRUCK FAMILY

The Firetruck Family consists of Jess and Dave and their daughters Poppy and Luna. Jess and Dave embraced vanlife with a young family, embracing living in the moment and reconnecting with nature and a simpler life while homeschooling Poppy and Luna on the road.

As a family we are passionate about and fascinated by upcycling, living low cost and alternative ways of living. We had a dream to convert a vehicle of our own which could comfortably fit a family of four while living and travelling. After a year of scrolling endless van advertisements, the firetruck popped up just twenty minutes away from us. She was a part of the Nottinghamshire fire service fleet and had been used to transport additional breathing apparatus to larger jobs. A bonus for us wasn't only the history of the van but that the fire service knows how to look after its vehicles. She came with only 40,000 miles on the clock too! The price was agreed and she was delivered to our drive the very next day.

The idea of a self-build all began back in 2015. We had two weeks, no plans and the thought of an all-inclusive holiday is our idea of a nightmare, so we threw our mattress and camping stove into our work van and travelled from Lincoln to St-Tropez. This journey ignited the idea of creating a van suited to our needs that would enable us to live more comfortably on the road and travel further.

For us, the necessities were an on-board loo and shower, cooking and food storage, and it had to have that home comfort feel about it too. We had a budget of roughly around £6,500 which, along with reclaiming and upcycling, we managed to stick to. Our biggest cost was ensuring the gas cylinder and electricity were fitted safely and to a certified standard. We also purchased a Truma Ultra store boiler and a underslung GAS-IT LPG cylinder. This enables us to have hot showers (Jess's luxury item), cook/store our food, run our on-board music system (Dave's luxury item) and our X2 175W solar panels. We installed a log burner too, which ticked off the home comfort element. Once we began our self-build, we came to the realisation that neither of us could actually drive the thing! Fully loaded, the truck weighs 5.5 tons so it was Dave's duty to step up and go through the terror of completing his CAT C licence. If he hadn't failed it the first time, we might have kept our cost under budget but we don't hold grudges in this family – usually!

Our conversion journey took us just under two years to complete. While juggling home/

work life we had our second baby Luna in the midst of the madness, so sometimes we were only able to work on the truck at weekends. Reclaiming and reusing stuff is important to us, so this added to our time as we felt it couldn't be rushed. A lot of the wood is salvaged from various areas; our pull-out table is reclaimed pitch pine from an old Methodist chapel and the work top in the kitchen came from a local sawmill. The bottle top splashback took us time to collect as our friends and family simply don't drink fast enough – our strict instructions to buy bottles with quirky tops probably didn't help! When converting the truck we realised that storage is key. With three girls who come with a lot of clothes on board it was vital we were able to store these away. The steps up to the main bed are even mini drawers! We fitted a tiny shower room with a composting loo, which took a lot of time to plan due to fitting it in such a compact space. Once we had finally completed it, we realised the shower tray was cracked and leaking! Ripping this area back out meant starting all over again. After four years of use this space is ready for a revamp, so very soon we will be spending some time and money on updating this little and much-needed area. We will definitely be considering a modern eco loo too!

With the truck finally completed we've enjoyed many trips away around the UK and staying in a new location each night is one of our favourite elements of this way of life. As a family,

we wanted to experience the real and raw reality of vanlife. We put our house on the market, sold all our belonging and took the plunge! At first we quietly resided in hidden woodland for several months and enjoyed true off-grid vanlife. Whilst spending time living in the woodland, we enjoyed homeschooling and rewilding with nature. We feel a child-led approach worked better for them and they learnt much more about themselves and their surroundings in that time.

Since then, we have had the opportunity to travel further. We travelled over 4,000 miles through Europe and spent time in the Scottish Highlands, experiencing the true value of vanlife and the opportunities this form of living has to offer. We have woken up in many different locations, from sea fronts to foots of mountains and sunrise at Stonehenge and so many more. Driving through the Italian Dolomites was probably one of our highlights and a place we plan to revisit. Waking up next the Riviera without paying the price for a 5-star hotel is perfection! For us, this way of living teaches our children the value of life: the basics like collecting twigs for the fire; the importance of the elements and nature and how to live alongside it; being close as a family; and spending precious time creating memories. All the things money cannot buy.

The future for the firetruck family is an exciting one – lots more travelling and living freely. Who knows, maybe relocating could be on the cards too. Stay tuned!

Follow Jess, Dave, Poppy and Luna's adventures on Instagram at firetruck.family.

THE FIRETRUCK FAMILY

Cost of conversion:	£6,500
Biggest outlay:	Having gas cylinder and electricity fitted safely and to a certified standard.
Best bargain:	Bottle top splashback made with collections from friends and family.
Useful feature:	Drawers within steps leading up to bed
Unforeseen cost:	Re-taking Cat C Licence
Ethos:	Spending precious time creating memories.

VEE VAN VOOM

Virginia Lowe is a retired massage therapist from Canada who decided at the age of 69 to build her van, Axel, and travel around the US.

I worked for thirty-eight years as a registered massage therapist and was blessed to have a work I loved. At 69 I decided to build my van and it was the first time I considered retirement. It took one year and most of the money I made that year to finish the build. Then, six months before my seventieth birthday, I retired. On 28 December 2019, I left Toronto for the US and the warmth of the south. I was on the road there for three months, mostly in Arizona, California and Oregon, then the coronavirus pandemic hit and I had to rush back to Canada as borders around the world closed down. I was lucky that it meant I was able to see my own country, Canada, which is magnificent and wild.

In 2018, a client of mine, Michelle, told me about watching YouTube and going 'down the rabbit hole' watching van builds. She felt it was better than Netflix. At the time I didn't give it much thought. Then a month or two later, there was nothing on TV I wanted to watch and I remembered the van thing and so gave it a look. I had a totally different reaction, what I felt was 'I can do this!' I think I was at a point in my life where I needed a challenge. Retirement seemed dull, but this meant freedom. I bought

the van out of my savings and paid for the build from my earnings.

I had designed and hired skilled people to help me renovate an ugly house in the past, so it seemed natural to do the same with Axel. I hired people to do complicated things, like solar installation, my Webasto installation and foam spray. I was lucky enough to have the help of good friends; my friend Robert did the wiring for me, my daughter help me cut the wood for the walls, Erich helped lay the floor, Ed taught me to make a template and James (canlifevanlife) did many difficult little things for me too. This van build took a village of kindness to create. I have also found that when something is beyond my skills while I am on the road, along comes just the right person who helps me out of the kindness of their heart. I find the vanlife community is very much like this.

Building a van is a bit like playing Tetris – a lot has to fit into a small space. It takes time to find a van, whether you buy new and wait for delivery, or you look for used which is downright complicated. It took me three months to find Axel. During that time, I researched what

I wanted by watching van builds on YouTube, looking at layouts, pricing and sizing up what I needed/wanted in my van. Since I didn't know the van size yet but believed a long one would be too hard to drive, I tried layouts that fit a short van. It quickly became apparent that it just would not fit nor could I afford everything. I made two lists: one for what I thought were needs and one that was clearly wants. I took the needs list and tried to work them into the layout, but I soon realised I did not need all these things – like a shower. I took a shower every day for years, but in a van you just can't carry that much water on board. So, no shower in my van but rather sponge baths and gym memberships! I went through this process hundreds of times until I bought my van and it dictated what I could really have now I had reduced my needs list. It turned out I bought the longest Ford Transit and got over my fear of driving a long vehicle. I just loved the double sliding doors that it came with.

I'm not really a budget person. I just know what I want and keep going until I have it. I used some money I inherited to buy Axel, my 2016 Ford Transit, which cost me CA$28,000 at the end of 2017. Then I worked for an extra year using all the money left over after bills, probably another $25,000 or $30,000. I found a lot of bargains along the way, including my antique copper wash tub, bought while in Portugal for less than half what it would cost at home, which I then took on the plane as my carry on. My most expensive luxury is my

ceiling, which is a faux tin roof. I priced up tin but it was way too expensive and would have rattled and driven me crazy, so I sourced these tiles that are hand painted to look old. They cost way too much, but I still love them!

My van is very spacious with only one upper cabinet, which gives it a lot of room around my head. I still need to design the garage under my bed. I'd like a few drawers and cubbies to hold my 'stuff' in place. Also, I plan on putting in a compost toilet at some point.

Nothing went wrong during the build – if anything broke it was fixed pretty quickly. This community of VanLifers is truly one of the most helpful I have ever experienced. It's sad that a lot of people just see us as homeless people that need to be shooed away. I still have a home that I have let my daughter live in, so I am not really 'homeless'. A lot of my friends have chosen this lifestyle after being hit by hardship, but we spend money in the towns we travel to and we pay taxes like everyone else. I feel it is time alternative lifestyles were encouraged, to both relieve the housing shortage and let people live the life they desire. We really are not hurting anyone if we park in your town for a night or two.

My friend Steph and I had met up for a few days at an old shipping lock on the St Lawrence. It was a gorgeous day, so we jumped off the side and swam, then we climbed up some rocks and walked back to the van. It was one of those perfect moments you get living in a van. I had dressed already, but Steph was just pulling up

her shorts when I heard her say, 'shit, here comes a cop.' A police officer walked between the vans and knocked on my van. I took a deep breath, put a smile on my face and said, 'hello', trying to think what we had done wrong. She asked, 'can I come in and see your van?' Whew! 'Of course,' I replied. She and her partner came in and spent the next half hour asking questions about the build and looking at the van. Apparently, she had been watching YouTube videos and wanted to build one for her and her kids. Steph, with quick thinking, asked the male officer, 'Can you tell me anywhere around here we could park for the night?' (We had been hoping to stay right where we were.) He answered, 'Any parking lot would be fine. *This* happens to be a parking lot.' We asked about the sign on the bridge that said no camping. He said, 'You aren't camping, you're parking overnight.' We spent the next two nights there.

I've had a similar experience at the border of the US when I've crossed the border and a guard has said they need to look in the van but they just really wanted to see the build!

I've been in my van for a year now and seen so many beautiful places that I'd love to return to. Sedona, Arizona, almost put me in a meditative trance as I hiked around red, oddly shaped rock formations. Then there was the Valley of Fire blazing a different red with its petrified wood and petroglyphs. Driving along the Pacific West Coast meant I saw hundreds of sea lions fighting and rolling on the beach, with the odd whale passing by and a huge eagle sitting on a sand bar. I love the wonder of pulling over and filling my soul with the beauty of the ocean, then making dinner and sleeping on the side of the road with the sounds of the waves to lull me to sleep.

I don't really plan my directions like one would on holidays. At the moment, with Covid on a spike upward, I'm hunkered down in Osoyoos, Okanagan Valley, British Columbia, Canada's only desert. There is very little of the virus here and it is gorgeous, but I am getting itchy feet and longing to see friends on the Island. Maybe that will be next. At the moment I am trying to learn how to make videos. I have a YouTube channel but it's a huge learning curve for a 70-year-old. I'm much better at Instagram because I love to post pictures of my travels.

Follow Virginia's adventures on Instagram at veevanvoom and on her YouTube channel.

AXEL

I've been blessed with help from:

@kage_and_ellie took a 4-hour drive out of their way through the mountains to meet up with me and fix my BIM when there was no sun for solar and boosting off the alternator was the only option.

@eric'sveganvan laid on the frozen ground under my van to install running boards because my leg and hip were inflamed from hauling myself up into the cabin.

Tannice Goddard painted the gorgeous design on my table in my outside kitchen, which can be seen when the table is in the upright position where it never fails to attract the admiration of fellow travellers. She paints from a deep spiritual place and this painting is of my personal journey. For more of her work check out her company Tannice Designs.

Mitch Baker of Baker Works Custom Woodworks built the cabinets in my van, which was a new endeavour for him. Van cabinets present a lot of challenges not encountered in house cabinets. He was brave enough to work it all out and even let me help him (which was probably no help at all).

Forest Stevens of Different Media is a videographer who specialises in van builds. He videoed my van in August 2020 as I started my journey across Canada. Forest has given me a voice in the van world.

Lisa Forret (@a.van.degroot) holds my camera or my hand as needed. Lisa and Jamie Forret are in my bubble as we all struggle to keep our sanity during these trying times.

DAPHNE THE PORTABLE POTTERY PALACE

Tasha Bee is a community artist based in Bristol who owns Pot Heads Pottery. She runs fun, relaxing pottery workshops that encourage social connection, creativity and a healthy dose of silliness! Her latest van conversion, Daphne, is a colourful mobile pottery studio that allows her to spread the pottery joy across the UK.

I don't live in my vehicle full-time, but it is equipped for me to live in for short periods when I am travelling around for work or adventuring! I have never liked staying in one place for too long, so having a home that roams suits me well. This is actually the third van that I have converted, they have got slightly bigger each time! The main purpose of this latest van, Daphne, is to allow me to travel with my business, Pot Heads Pottery. The van is a Portable Pottery Studio, allowing me to deliver my pottery workshops all over the country and beyond! I take it to festivals and events, as well as harder-to-reach rural communities. I want to make creative play accessible to people of all ages, abilities and backgrounds and The Pot Head workshops are designed to introduce people to pottery in a really fun and sociable way.

I am in many online groups and have quite a few friends who live, or have lived, in vans over the years. There are some incredible self-builds out there, so that was very inspiring. I also love the '70s/mid-century aesthetic and that has been a big inspiration for me in my build.

I love making things, upcycling and DIY. Doing a full conversion on a van has been a dream of mine for quite a while. I am also very particular and know what I want once I have an idea in my mind, so I just couldn't have let anyone else do it really! I had quite a clear aesthetic vision for this project and have loved the process of bringing it into reality – I've learned a lot along the way. There are still quite a few bits and pieces that I want to do to it as well, so it's a bit of an ongoing project.

There are a lot of behind-the-scenes parts that you have to get done before you can do the more exciting bits you can actually see when it's finished. Firstly, it's about choosing a base vehicle that is sound and is going to last. In my case, as I chose an older vehicle, I had to spend quite a bit of time making sure any rusty bits were dealt with and that it was all mechanically sound. It's not much fun spending big chunks of your budget on things like welding and bodywork, but it is worth it in the long run. The next big job that you don't get to see (but is definitely essential) is insulation. I insulated Daphne with an eco-friendly insulation board all over, which took quite a bit of time and effort — not to mention lots of glue-in-hair scenarios — but now she's super toasty in the winter, and stays cool in the summer too. Other things I had to think about were how I was going to lay out the furniture, and what materials I could use that wouldn't add too much weight to the build. Then finally there were the fun bits like the colour scheme and what fabrics to use! I actually chose a '70s-style floral print fabric for the curtains, which I found on eBay and felt really drawn to for some reason — turns out it was the same material that was in my granny and grandad's kitchen! My grandad was a sculptor and he got me into pottery when I was a little girl, so it felt very fitting.

I actually ran a Crowdfunder campaign to raise funds to build the Portable Pottery Studio. My target was £3,000 and I raised just over that. It was awesome that so many people got behind my idea and it gave me a real boost to get the project on the road — excuse the pun! By the time I have completely finished the project, I will probably have spent about £5,000 in total. I have saved money by upcycling a lot of bits and pieces, and by building my own furniture from scrap bits of wood and skip raiding. The colourful cabinet was rescued from my mum and dad's shed and painted up, and I have also re-used some of the old bits of ply that were in

the van originally. The biggest expense is probably going to be the electrical system, though I actually managed to get some second-hand solar panels for a really good price. I like the idea of the van allowing me to be off-grid and using solar power when I need electricity. I spent about £250 on spray paint for the exterior, which felt a little excessive at the time, but I am so glad that I did because I love how it came out — full flower-power vibes!

I think the most unique thing about Daphne is her colourful paint job! I sometimes forget when I'm driving around in her and wonder why people are looking at me with a funny smile on their faces — then I remember that I'm in a big flowery van! My dad helped me to prep the van for painting, and we took the 'TRANSIT' badge at the back off but it fell apart in the process. When we went to put it back on, we put it on backwards so now it says 'TRA ISNT' — I think it's quite fitting!

Obviously, with the idea being that it is both a Portable Pottery Studio and a camper/live-in vehicle, I have had to be quite creative with how I use the space. I have tried to make it as adaptable as possible by using things like the pegboard above the cabinet, which can be easily changed from a kitchen-type area to a workshop space to hold tools. The area at the back also transforms from a seating area with a table, able to host a workshop for four people, to a double bed. This took some careful planning and quite a lot of head scratching!

Overall, I'm pretty happy with the build so far, though I'm wondering if I will ever feel like

it is completely finished. I still have so much more that I want to do! I think if I were to do it again, I might choose a slightly taller vehicle, and I am planning to add more over-head storage to improve the space even more. You can never have enough storage really, especially when you accumulate things at the rate that I do!

I love my long shelf just for plants, with its wibbly-wobbly edge; it's not for everyone, but I love it! I also really like that Daphne runs on Petrol/LPG rather than diesel. It's quite a rare find and although LPG can be hard to come by, when you can fill up it is half the price and

much better for the environment too. I also really like the fact that there is storage above the cab as it's a really good use of space.

Living in Bristol, I am very blessed to be surrounded by so much wonderful countryside to travel in. I grew up in Brighton and love to be by the sea, so anywhere on the coast is appealing for me. I often travel to Wales (when we are able to!) and I love it there. Hopefully, when things get moving again, I will be able to take the van on a little tour and run some workshops in different locations. I would like to take her to some events and spread the pottery joy across the UK!

Follow Tasha and Daphne's adventures on Instagram at potheads.pottery and learn more about the studio and workshops at her website peacefulpots.bigcartel.com.

DAPHNE

I would like to say a huge thank you to my dad, Mark. It was an absolute dream to be able to work on the van together and it turned out to be the silver lining of us all being in lockdown over the summer of 2020. I loved spending that time together working on the van, and I hope he enjoyed it too. I will always think of him whenever I take it anywhere and I wouldn't have been able to do half of it without him ... So thanks Dad (and thanks Mum for all the cups of tea!). Also to all my friends who have helped out with different parts of building it. I love that when I look around I can remember all of the people who were a part of putting it all together.

MARIE GARRATT

Marie, Ash and their border collie, Bolski, travel in convoy across Europe in two matching green Ivecos. With a passion for film and photography, they document their travels as they go.

The truth is that I never actually planned on living in a van full-time, but that quickly changed when I discovered how fun, freeing and exciting the lifestyle was. Everything about it just makes sense, and it still does now. With a passion for travel and photography, converting a van allowed me to do the things I loved, at the same time exploring an alternative lifestyle – that's not to say it's easy though. You're likely to come across challenges that will make you question everything, but you just have to deal with them one at a time, like anything else.

My first campervan was a 1993 Talbot Express. I fell head over heels for its quirky look, and its everything-I-could-ever-need interior; I was completely sold. I convoyed with a friend (now my partner) to the French Alps for the winter season. We got jobs, learnt to ski and had the time of our lives, but I soon realised that this vehicle was not living material, especially in winter. There was little insulation and only a small gas heater, so everything froze as we were in below-zero temperatures. When I returned to the UK for its MOT, I realised I had been swindled.

At this point I was fully invested in living in a van and as my family home was to be sold soon, I was essentially homeless. I sold the Talbot and everything I had of value, including my car, to fund the next vehicle which would be made to my specific wants and needs. I managed to pull together £3,000 to fund it all. The foundations and interior of the van such as insulation, solar, gas, electrics and so on came to roughly £1,500, leaving me with the same budget for the van itself.

I mentioned at the beginning the challenges you may come across that will make you question it all, and those will probably come up in the early stages when you're learning everything. But for me, the biggest challenge was a unique situation which relied on precise organisation. With my partner still in France, it was our aim to get everything needed for the build and drive back over to the Alps where the build would take place. I aimed to do the drive in one go, but you soon realise that when on the road that not an awful lot goes to plan – be prepared for that. What started off as an exciting race to the finish line, soon turned into an impossible mission with endless wrong turns, anxiety attacks and nowhere to sleep but the cab – was it really all worth it? Eventually, I arrived back in Chamonix with my dog Bolski, who had managed to keep me sane.

From then on, the build took place in one of the most beautiful carparks, surrounded by a 360-degree view of the Alps. Powered by the solar on Ash's van and an excessive collection of tools, we managed to get the vehicle liveable in around two weeks. Thanks to us having all of the building materials needed and a plan in mind, it was really a case of just building it. As we were building it in on the road we didn't have much time to complete it, so for that reason my skilled partner (Ash) did the majority of the build. This meant I could watch and learn the whole process, and be there to help when needed. We were short of a few tools here and there but made do with what we had at the time. So if we can build a whole van with the tools that we had on us, powered only by the sun, then no matter how skilled you are or what few tools you have, building your own van can absolutely be achieved. All it requires is a little research and patience!

Nearly two years after the build, the van is still going strong and has been my permanent home ever since. The exterior has had a splash of colour to match Ash's van when in convoy. From season to season I've adapted and acquired additions that make it suitable to live in all year round; from bikinis to skis, I've got it all. I recently discovered candle making, which are all handmade in the van itself. I make and

sell these as I travel, which helps with some of my living costs. For a long time, I had all of the equipment in a big box, which wasn't ideal. So I ended up compromising on a little space so I could fit in some plastic drawers to hold what I needed. I think it's such a brilliant thing that living in a home completely suited to your lifestyle means that it's easy to change or adapt it to match your needs.

With that being said, changes are inevitable. You've most likely heard the phrase that 'It's never finished', and it's true. Originally, I had a step through to my cab seats which Bolski could easily jump on to, but I soon tired of this and have now completely pulled it out so there is a simple walkway. It means he can't jump up on to the cab seats anymore, but in his old age I think it's better for him anyway. Even after all this time little things that I want to change have been building up slowly. This has now resulted in quite a big change around, and the bed area has now been adjusted to an L-shaped seating area which pulls out into a bed. I've had to lose a lot of garage space to enable this, but not having somewhere to sit and enjoy a cuppa gets very annoying. I didn't realise it for a long time but once I did, it was always there in the back of my mind. It now also means my van is a lot more sociable and I can seat guests if needed. However, the main reason for this design change was to fit in a log burner. Ash and I love exploring colder climates, and after surviving our first Scandinavian winter in the north of Sweden when his log burner undoubtedly kept us going throughout the challenging months –

without it we would have had to travel south. I don't have my own log burner yet, but I already know it's going to be my favourite feature in the van. For now though, my favourite part has to be the kitchen. I love its narrowboat feel with the portholes, and when the evening sun is shining through, it's really just beautiful.

It's hard to say where my favourite place I've travelled to is; each country I've visited has its own unique beauty spots. Some countries are not so accepting of life on the road while others are a lot easier. While most people opt for warmer climates, my favourite time has always been during the winter months. If you can learn to love the winter months as much as the summer ones, your possibilities will be endless. Although it's God's gift to be able to sit with your doors open, basking in the sun and surrounded by nature, it's an even rarer gift to feel like you're the only one driving through the country. Scotland is a must-see for many people, and when we explored in the winter months, my only regret was not visiting sooner. A lot of places might be closed, but the roads will be all yours to explore completely.

Our latest venture has been exploring Sweden. To think that we've driven our self-converted vans from the UK to the North of Sweden to live beneath the Northern lights absolutely blows our minds. We've enjoyed being here so much that we've decided to purchase some land and build an off-grid homestead here, gathering everything we've learned from building the vans and applying it to a permanent home. With all the recent travel restrictions that have come into place due to Brexit and the coronavirus pandemic, we feel there's no better time to stay put and work on this exciting new project. In the future, this will be our base, somewhere we can safely return to after our trips and a place to call our own.

The word vanlife is so much more than it lets on. It begins another a chapter in life and introduces you to a whole other world.

○ Follow Marie, Ash and Bolski's adventures on Instagram at mariegarratt_ and on Marie's blog www.marielouisegarratt.com, where you can also buy her beautiful handmade candles. You can also watch their videos on YouTube at their channels Lost in Europe and Marie Garratt.

MARIE

Favourite season:	Winter – if you can learn to love the winter months as much as the summer ones, your possibilities will be endless.
Favourite feature:	My narrowboat style kitchen with its portholes.
Future must-have:	Log burner to keep me warm on our travels.
Must-see place:	Scotland
Next adventure:	Building an off-grid base in Sweden beneath the Northern Lights.

CAMPER VIBE

Lou and Em started chauffeuring their dog, AJ, around the world in 2017. However, after deciding the first van was not big enough for him, AJ had the girls embark on a second luxury conversion – far more suited to an adventure dog on the road!

We have both travelled since the age of 16 and have always had a passion for the great outdoors, with everything it has to offer from beautiful landscapes and cascading waterfalls to the amazing people you meet along the way. This shared passion was something that drew us together and we continued to travel, starting out in a tent as our first home together in Cornwall. From there, our family grew. We upgraded to a house, but still wanted to travel. We continued to camp in a tent, but when we got AJ we soon found out that he is a bit of a hunter and escape artist. So, I (Em) was paranoid that he would hear a rabbit or fox in the night and chew his way out of the tent. I would make poor Lou tether AJ to her just in case, so we decided something a little more robust would work better!

Plus, due to us wanting to go on extended trips, the security and mobility from our all-weather build means we can experience full-time travel far more comfortably and with the freedom we have always wanted.

When we made the decision to upgrade, we went to so many forecourts to look at vans and motorhomes, but at that point we had two large dogs, and we wanted as much floor space as possible and the prebuilt ones just did not cut it. That is when the idea of doing it ourselves popped into our heads – plus, throughout our entire relationship we have never shied away from a challenge and this seemed like a perfect one for us to undertake together. If you do it yourself, you can have so much more fun deciding what goes where, colour schemes, materials used to build – the choices are endless.

Layout, layout, and layout – that was the biggest thing for us. We wanted the floor space to be as large as possible due to having AJ; not many other vans have the amount of floor space that we do in ours. After this, we faced the usual torment of which van to buy, a huge deal when embarking upon a self-build. Wanting a fixed bed along the width against the back helped narrow the search down to three types of vans: Boxer, Relay or Ducato. Lou is 5ft 7in and just fits with the insulation and cladding due to these types of vans being more box-shaped rather than narrowing towards the top of the van.

'A few nights in the Sierra Nevada, tucked up all warm in bed, looking at the stars, made cutting the extra holes in the van worth it.'

Then came the difficulty of balancing which products and accessories would work best for us against cost – you could easily spend your life's savings building the perfect van.

Having experienced a smaller basic van previously, we knew we wanted a full kitchen and a full oven with hobs was a must. I know people like to cook outdoors – as do we – but as we wanted to travel all year round we needed to have the option of cooking inside the van, and I must say my van oven is better than my house oven!

Our initial budget was £14,000 for the van and the conversion. Unfortunately, as with most builds, we blew the budget clean out of the water. We spent £14,000 on the conversion alone, and the van itself cost us £7,000 on top of that. Our biggest bargain was most likely our cupboards, which were made completely from recycled/reclaimed wood and coffee sacks we had been hoarding for quite some time with our build in mind. Our most expensive luxury were our windows; we could have got cheaper ones, but I (Em) wanted fly nets, so we went with Seitz windows.

We found the coffee sacks when we had our first little van and we knew that we wanted to incorporate them into the new build with the pallet wood. It kind of started from that really, we knew we wanted a highly functional but rustic-looking van.

We did go through a fair few trial tins of varnish and wood stains, then sanding them back, starting again to find the exact right shade.

Sometimes it can look a little too dark and as we wanted the blue we knew we needed the wood to be a mixture of lighter stain and white to give the impression of more space.

Lou's passion for wildlife photography and our joint love of nature influenced the number of windows; we wanted one in all four sides so we had a panoramic view of our surroundings, and as good a chance of taking in the local wildlife of whatever country we were parked in. We spent some time at the observatory in Kielder Forest. Seeing how beautiful the sky and stars can be made the decision to fit a skylight above our bed an easy one. A few nights in the Sierra Nevada, tucked up all warm in bed, looking at the stars, made cutting the extra holes in the van worth it.

Pretty much all went well (Lou is a carpenter and researches the hell out of everything, and that helped) apart from fitting the solar. Lou stupidly cut off the labels, so then she didn't know what went where – that was a bit of a nightmare. Apart from that, and the odd bit of insulation stuck to our skin, the build went relatively smoothly. I think the fact that this was our second van conversion really helped us every step of the way.

We are very glad that we put in swivel seats as they are great for extra space and seating and they are definitely our favourite feature of the van. We love the fact that if we pull up somewhere and it's raining we can spin round and be straight into our living space without a wet boot or muddy paw in sight.

'The list of our favourite places could go on and on.'

As for something we wished we had, a pop-up shower would be ideal. We did not want a full one due to wanting more space, but we are planning on installing a pop-up shower for when it is colder outside.

We used Autogas 2000 and Barratt Tanks for our underslung LPG tank, water and waste tanks, the rest was us. Lou was adamant she wanted to give as much of the build as possible a go herself, including the dreaded electrics!

Having the van has enabled us to visit some amazing places that we would not normally have seen; we recently embarked on a trip through France and into Spain. We explored a lot of inland Spain, which was amazing. It has beautiful countryside and amazing wildlife – something that you would not expect of Spain. For our first adventure in the van out of the UK, we found using the local Aires really easy. Using the Park4Night app really helped and the reviews that people gave, to which we of course added, gives you a great insight into each area.

We did, however, have a fairly big breakdown whilst in Spain and ended up having our van towed back to the UK. It's a long story but we did document all of it on our YouTube channel, and I really think if we didn't have the channel and a reason to film and keep going it would have made that whole experience a lot worse – that and AJ, of course; he got us through it as well.

Within the UK, Lou absolutely loves travelling to the New Forest; the wildlife there and the endless woodland walks keep her busy for days. I, however, prefer the tranquillity that can be found sitting beside the river in the Wye Valley; listening to the sound of water flowing, with a good book and a bit of sunshine, is the perfect way to spend an afternoon.

As for further afield, we are both well-travelled but could probably agree that Mexico is one of our favourite places and would love to ship the van there one day, although to be honest, the list of our favourite places could go on and on.

We have a pretty big Europe trip planned, though with the way the world is right now we may have to settle for a circular trip of the UK. If we do make it over to Europe, the place we are looking forward to visiting the most is Romania, as we very much want to see bears and wolves in the wild.

Follow Lou, Em and AJ's adventures on Instagram at camper_vibe and on their YouTube channel. See more of Lou's wildlife photography on Instagram at louisestockbridge.

CAMPER VIBE

Biggest consideration: Layout
Cost of van: £7,000
Cost of conversion: £14,000
Biggest luxury: Seitz windows
Biggest bargain: Cupboards made of reclaimed wood and coffee sacks.
Favourite feature: Swivel seats – spinning straight into our living room when we pull up!
Future must-have: Pop-up shower

Park4Night is an app that allows you to find and share locations for relaxing or parking up in your camper, your equipped van or normal van. You can look at places shared by others; the app will guide you to them and comments from other users tell you about facilities and nearby activities.

FLORRY THE LORRY

SMALL home BIG adventure: Chris and Cat live in their converted lorry, Florry, with their chocolate Labrador, Rolo. With their blended family of five children, it was too extravagant to stay in hotels during holidays, so they opted to buy a motorhome. This was the start of their life exploring the world in a tiny home on wheels. They were much more at home in the wilderness, camping and exploring nature together than staying in hotels and so the idea of a self-built home came to mind.

We were working crazy hours to maintain our home of bricks and mortar in London. Chris' job in IT was demanding and the price of things increased every year. With the work/life balance tipping heavily towards the working end, it wasn't a healthy lifestyle. The timing was right to make the big move to living a simpler, healthier life. It was a difficult decision and at times very scary, but we knew we weren't able to continue as we were – financially or emotionally.

We spent a lot of time discussing how we could have a simpler life. Chris wasn't in favour of living full-time in a motorhome as, in his words, 'they're designed for a short holiday and the odd weekend away.' Having owned one, we felt that a bought off-the-peg motorhome was not up to full-time living and living off-grid for long periods of time.

In 2017, we were on a scuba diving holiday in Menorca and discovered one of the instructors actually lived full-time in her converted 7.5-tonne lorry. This was the inspiration we needed. We were so excited that instead of compromising about what we wanted, we could build our own home and have exactly what we needed. The added bonus was that making it ourselves meant we would know exactly how everything works, and how to fix it ourselves if something went wrong. Building a home on wheels meant we could combine our passion for travel and diving, as well as living a simpler life.

With Chris working in IT and Catherine as a teacher, both of us were new to self-builds, but we embraced the challenge. Life is short and converting a lorry to live in full-time would lead to a simpler and less stressful life.

We had a lot to think about, including design, what vehicle to buy and where we could do the build. We finally found an available DAF LF45 7.5-tonne lorry. We had realised that with our large dog and scuba equipment that we needed more than a 3.5-tonne van. We made a deal with the buyer to keep the lorry on his

'We felt like giving up several times, but each time we motivated each other, and we got through it together.'

land while we did the conversion, as parking on London roads to work on her would have been impossible!

We came up with the design for our beautiful conversion over many hours spent at a kitchen table drawing and redrawing, and watching endless blogs on YouTube. We even made a little mini cardboard cut-out to scale! Finally, we used a software programme called Sketch Up. Little by little, with Cat's planning and Chris vision as well as lots of blood, sweat and tears, Florry began to take shape.

Due to cost, there was never any question about someone else doing the build aside from the tricky installation of a gas tank which was done by a qualified person with the proper certification for gas installations.

We were both working full-time jobs so were only able to work on it every other weekend, and occasionally a late evening through the week. We felt like giving up several times, but each time we motivated each other, and we got through it together. After eighteen months of hard slog the build was complete, but now we had our home with us wherever we wanted to go, which made the gruelling hours and hard work worth it.

We hired Jonathan Horton, who manufactures roof racks, doors, stairs etc. for self-build trucks, to make our electric stairs and steel door. We used many types of wood, including 50mm pine for the structure, and then recycled old pallet wood, tongue and groove bits and bobs for shelving and other features.

Florry has a proper kitchen and plumbing system with a 336l water tank, a comfortable bed, and two large solar panels for energy. It's been designed how we wanted it, with a kitchen slightly higher than normal as we are both very tall. We also designed Florry so that Rolo would have his own unique bed under ours, not that he uses it a lot as he seems to prefer the sofas and our bed – now there's a surprise!

We believe that building a home on wheels is harder than a (static) tiny home, as we had to consider the weight and the fact that there would be a lot of movement when on the road.

Our best buy and the one that gives us the most pleasure is our little Hobbit wood-burning stove. We got a bargain as it was second hand for £200 – new with a flue they are almost £1,000. We also got a caravan for £400 that we stripped for its windows along with a few other little bits and bobs. The rest of the caravan was used by our friends to build a moveable chicken coop. The most expensive feature is our fridge-freezer which cost over £1,000, but we're very happy with it and it gets a lot of use. We have an amazing compost toilet, which we were given by Kildwick Composting Toilets.

We bought Florry for £15,500 and spent another £10,000–£15,000 on the build. To buy a motorhome of this size would have cost us more than £90,000. We are proud to have been able to build ourselves a beautiful home on wheels for a fraction of the cost it would have been to buy one and can live a simpler and more environmentally friendly life.

'We can take joy in a beautiful sunset in the countryside, or a charming medieval village found on a drive.'

If we could go back in time, we would change where we installed the skylights as the kitchen is a little dark. We would also extend the bathroom just a little. When we get back to the UK, we plan to cut the back doors in half to allow the top to open from the inside and the bottom from outside so we don't have to open all of it when we want to enjoy some fresh air and beautiful views from our bedroom.

In 2019, after lots of hard work, the build was finished and we were finally able to spend eight months in our new home, living abroad and touring with Rolo. We have found places to park fairly easily in Europe, as there are more sites available there than in the UK, and on our travels we have experienced many interesting things – both good and bad.

One time we got lost in the Spanish mountains on a windy road leading to nowhere. When we got to the top, after much struggle and feeling a little unsure on the roads, we were met by a very kind man who let us stay on his land. Not only did he offer us a place to park up safely, he had a beautiful pool to use and water to refill our tanks. Out of an adverse situation came some good!

We've had a few bad experiences as well, such as breaking down a couple of times and once when a crazy man in Belgium tried to ram Florry because he didn't want us parking next to him.

Life on the road is often over-glamorised. In reality it's hard, but it's still been so much better for us than life in a city, working all

hours and trying to keep up with the life we had. We made the choice to live this way – we don't have the luxuries of long hot showers, we always need to think about our next water fill up, winter is hard and we don't have the luxury of flushing toilets. But we do have a much simpler, cheaper life where we can explore and combine our passions to dive and travel. We don't miss any of the materialistic things, we just miss a bath from time to time!

While travelling, we can take joy in a beautiful sunset in the countryside, or a charming medieval village found on a drive. We're happy with the richness of nature and the outdoor life, and the benefits this brings to our life. Cat's favourite place is where she leaves a part of her heart each time she leaves – Menorca, where we love diving in the crystal-clear water. France is another favourite place as Cat is half French and has a lot of family there. It also offers everything – mountains, lakes, sea, medieval cities, countryside and good food and wine. What more could anyone ask for? We have met many wonderful and friendly people along our journey and feel very much a part of the vanlife community who all look out for each other. It's a great caring community to be a part of.

We were supposed to be working as campsite wardens in 2020 but then the coronavirus pandemic struck; luckily Cat's dad let us stay on his drive until we could head off again. Once restrictions lifted, we headed back to our life on the road. Sadly, the coronavirus pandemic has meant that the start of 2021 has been harder,

with more restrictions on travel and borders closing, but we hope that will change soon so we can spend time with our families.

As of January 2021, we are in Menorca; due to the curfews in France and the lockdown in the UK, we felt it was safer to stay here until things ease. When things improve, we would like to visit Eastern Europe, Scandinavia, Turkey and Greece – not all in one trip but slowly and with time and space to do so. We'd also love to take Florry to Canada, though it will take a lot of saving to afford that.

Follow Chris, Cat, Rolo and Florry's adventures on Instagram at florrythelorry, as well as Facebook, YouTube, TikTok and Twitter, and check out their website www.florrythelorry.com.

FLORRY

Build Tips

- Buy half a dozen tape measures and a box of pencils – otherwise you'll spend half your build looking for one or the other.
- Put your plumbing where you can reach it. We started with the pipes in the floor and after almost putting a screw through one, we decided to rip them out and put them under the vehicle.
- Use wires that are far too big for what you need and are not behind everything so you can access them. If you want to add a light or a USB socket or something after you can T off the existing cable, not have to run another one.
- Make everything 12V Inverters which convert 12V to mains power aren't 100 per cent efficient – at best they are 85 per cent efficient – so if you use 12V for an inverter and then use it to charge your mobile then you're wasting 15 per cent of the energy converting from one power type to another. It's much better to use a 12V cigarette lighter socket and buy a 12V charger for your laptop/mobile/tablet etc.
- Buy an electric screwdriver as well as a drill. We have one by Ryobi which can charge by USB. It saves you a lot of time when you don't have to swap your drill bit for a screwdriver head every thirty seconds.
- Keep weight in mind with everything you do. We're lucky, the unladen weight of a DAF LF45 is 3.4 tonnes, so we had 4.1 tonnes to use – even so we weigh in at almost 7 tonnes. A Mercedes Sprinter medium wheelbase has a maximum weight of 3.5 tonnes. But its 'kerb weight' (which is basically empty) is 2.1 tonnes, leaving you with just 1.4 tonnes and remember that you want to come in well under your weight so you have 1,000kg to use on your build.

Design Tips:

- Get the biggest water tank you can – your gas will usually last a month, your solar will keep your batteries charged, but your water will always run out before anything else.
- If you are using gas bottles make sure you can fit European tanks in the locker – they are generally shorter and wider than the UK variety.
- If you are going to use LPG then get a proper gas engineer to fit one. This is one of the few jobs we didn't do ourselves as we needed to be sure it was safe. Design your solar system for the worst days. In the UK the shortest day is 7 hours 49 minutes, and you won't get much power if the sun is low in the sky. Make sure you have at least a 1:1 ratio, if possible 2:1, so 200W solar to 100W batteries; this will make sure you have power on the worst days.

Travel Tips:

- Always fill up with water and LPG when you can – even if you have three-quarters of a tank, fill it up when passing garages or Aires.
- If you're travelling in Europe then make sure you have a set of LPG adapters. We have one for France and Italy, but not a Spanish one. Luckily, in every garage we've used they have a box of adapters and they let us borrow one.
- We have a rule of 'if it's not used after twelve months, it goes' (this excludes essentials like breakdown equipment etc.). You'd be surprised by how much stuff is at the back of the cupboard that you never use anymore!
- Always make sure when travelling to a destination that you have an alternative nearby. We've arrived at places a few times and we either didn't like them or they were closed, and we had to find an alternative. If you've chosen to go somewhere, make sure there's a second location close by where you can park up instead.

Relationship Tips

- Always respect each other's own time and space. Space in a van is limited, but it's always possible to go out and give each other space when needed. Life in a van can be challenging at times when you're cooped up all day and night together. Find time to discuss things you need to talk about, respect each other and be kind.
- Life in a van means you can't be shy about using the toilet in front of your partner! There are many hang ups you will have to let go of. I have had to shave my legs sitting on a toilet with Chris working next to me.
- Sometimes life on the road can feel isolated. Keep in contact with family and friends via whatever technology you have available.

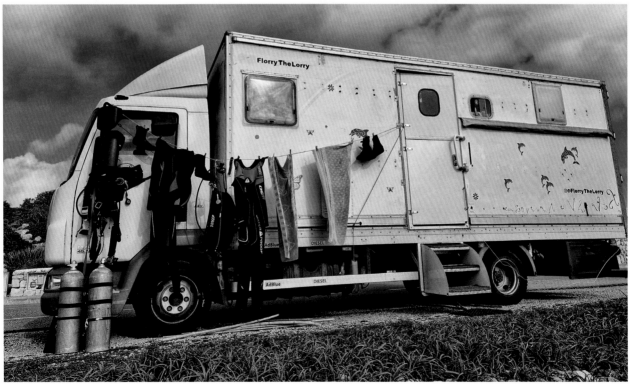

THOSE WEIRDOS

Dom, Missy and daughter Rosie have travelled around in the Sub with their two cats and two dogs since 2019. Dom is the Captain of the Sub; Missy is Navigator and Head Chef; Rosie is an artist and gamer and runs her own jewellery-making business from the van.

Dom and Missy work online, originally promoting nightclub events but since Covid they've been creating other revenue streams from YouTube, Amazon affiliate marketing, writing a recipe e-book and creating T-shirt designs.

It all began in the summer of 2018. I had discovered #vanlife on Instagram and had happily browsed the images of adventure and cosy tiny homes on wheels for hours. When I brought the concept up with Dom, he said he'd heard of vanlife and that travelling in a campervan was already on his bucket list!

We quite often have mad little ideas – most fall by the wayside after some discussion, but some stick. The idea of getting rid of almost everything we owned and living in a van stuck!

We found our long wheelbase high top Sprinter van (the Sub) in September 2018, spent eight months converting it (while also running our two businesses, a couple of Girl Guide units, and selling and packing up our entire houseful of stuff).

It would be Dom and I, our 10-year-old daughter Rosie, and Dom's 16-year-old son Phoenix. Phoenix planned to come with us, taking a gap year between secondary school and college, but after travelling for a while he decided to head back to the UK where his girlfriend and friends were. He's at college now and is contemplating getting a van of his own for surfing trips!

We set off for Europe on 17 June 2019 and travelled until we got stuck in the UK lockdown in March 2020. We escaped again in June and spent six happy months on Spanish beaches before getting stuck in the UK again after coming back for Christmas! We're now working on a plan to get land and residency in Portugal to get around the Brexit travel restrictions.

We knew from the off that we wanted to convert a van ourselves. We had fairly unique requirements as we needed beds, seats and storage for four people, plus two cats and two dogs. We also liked the idea of being able to make each part bespoke, and we love a challenge!

The main thing we had to base our build around was the four humans living in a van problem. We needed three full-size beds – a double and two singles. We decided that all the beds would move out of the way to create a seating area in the day, so the kids' singles went on the bottom. One side slides over and the mattress was split so it could become a backrest. Then the upper double bed has pulleys and boat winches so it rises up into the ceiling, allowing enough space to sit upright underneath.

We also needed to add a pair of seats in the back because our van only had two in the front plus the driver's seat. Everything else just had to squeeze in around that! We built a waterproof room with a drain in the floor to house our compost toilet, so we can shower in there if it's too cold outside. We crammed a large fridge (110L) under the hob and a large LPG bottle under the sink. We'd rather have had the gas under the van, but there just wasn't room with our two water tanks and spare tyre under there already.

We have utilised every scrap of space for storage – pans fit in the dead space behind the seats and vegetables live in a basket under the bed. We put an overcab shelf in and kept a space at the back of the van for our folding chairs, BBQ and boxes of tinned food.

The pets were another consideration. We built a cat litter tray cubby under our drawers, with a removable front for cleaning. We also created a special box in the sliding door footwell to house dog toys. The lid flips out at night to cover the well, so Bogie doesn't fall down it! Juan and the cats sleep on the bed with us. We also screwed a scratching mat to the kitchen cupboard door – although the cats seem to prefer using the seat covers!

We spent a long time looking at pictures of van interiors, trying to decide how we wanted ours to look. We were quite taken with the idea of having a beachy vibe – lots of turquoise and white, a sandy colour on the floor, driftwood and gauzy white curtains. We also considered making the interior look like a real submarine with lots of stainless steel, rivets and red wheel valves. Although this would have looked epic and totally unique, it wouldn't have been very cosy!

In the end we decided it would be most joyful to fill the Sub with colour. We started out using the Beatles' Yellow Submarine artwork as inspiration, which then turned into a mad vibrant colour palette – lots of bright orange, yellow, pink, red and blue. We absolutely love it and wouldn't change a thing!

If I could go back and redo the conversion, there are definitely a lot of things I'd do differently! For a start, I'd make the electrical cupboard easier to access. I didn't realise how often I would need to get to things to check on or replace things. I wouldn't bother making the beds move around as we haven't used that setup for over a year; I would have just added the swivel to the front seats at the start. And I would have cladded the walls instead of using sheets of ply – to keep the build light!

We have a few all-time favourite features on the Sub. We fitted a skylight over our bed after a year and it was a total game changer. It lets the morning light in right over our faces; we

sleep with it wide open when it's hot, and the cats love sitting under it too. It brings a lot of light into what was a dark cave at the back of the van. Magic!

Fitting the swivel on the front seats has meant that we can create a seating area right by the sliding door and open up the space, making it feel much roomier.

Our floor-to-ceiling spice rack is the feature most commented on by visitors. We built it into the stud wall of the wet room by not adding ply to the outside – a clever use of otherwise wasted space!

We've upgraded the van a few times already; we added the skylight and upgraded from a plastic loo to a much more solid wooden one – we highly recommend Strumpet and Trollop! We have other upgrades planned – I'd love to switch to LI04 batteries, increase from 300ah to 600ah, add a second B2B charger and a tilting rack to our solar panel. Electricity shortage is our biggest concern in the van. We also plan to convert one of the lower beds into extra storage space as it's currently unused space.

We have amassed a few tales to tell around the campfire from our eighteen months on the road ...

There's the one about our elderly dog who started leaking every night, who now has to wear nappies held together with gaffer tape. Then there was the time in France when we drove for four hours only to end up half an hour away from the Eurotunnel because we'd been going in circles. One time we sank wheel deep in soft silt and had to be pulled out by a Spanish farmer on his tractor – while fifty locals watched and cackled at us. Another time, Dom nearly lost an eye when a bungee cord snapped up and hit him in the face ... so many stories.

We've seen some epic wildlife too: chameleons, dolphins, storks, flamingos, a terrapin, mad-looking beetles, bats, ibex, hoopoes, beavers, boar, octopuses, pilot whales and lots more.

Our favourite place to visit is Orgiva, Andalusia. It has a bohemian atmosphere, hippy craft markets, a campsite for emergencies (showers and electricity), a lady who makes pizza and bread by hand and delivers right to the van, a beautiful stand of eucalyptus trees to park under, and a lovely town full of fab shops and several vegan eateries ... it's no wonder Orgiva is our favourite town in the whole of Spain!

Our current future looks like a permaculture homestead in Portugal, while we wait for Covid travel restrictions to ease up. We're not done travelling yet!

Follow Dom, Missy and Rosie's adventures on Instagram at wearethoseweirdos, at their website www.thoseweirdos.online and on their YouTube channel.

THE SUB

Converting Tips

- Don't use screw end breakers. Always use the more expensive ones that need crimp ends on the cables.
- Make sure you can access things after the build, e.g. the back of the fridge to clean the compressor; the cable runs in case you want to add new electricals; the top of the diesel heater in case you need to change a glow plug ...
- Measure it five times, cut once!

Travelling Tips

- Fill up with water every chance you get, don't wait until you're nearly empty. You never know when you'll next see a tap!
- Check your wheel nuts are tight every so often – ours got loose and destroyed a wheel!
- Stay a while if you find a nice spot. When you see the sun rising each day it gives you a real connection to the land and the way the weather affects your surroundings. We only learned this after a year of travelling fast, always moving on after a day or two. We spent seven weeks on the same beach and it was eye opening.
- Keep relevant spares in the van – a glow plug for your heater, a wing mirror, wiper blades etc. You never know when you'll need something. Actually, you can have a pretty good guess – it'll be when you're in the middle of nowhere, at night, on a Sunday so everything's shut ...

GOING BOUNDLESS

Robbie and Priscilla are based in Florida. Inspired by tiny homes and their love of travel, they decided to convert a school bus so that they could travel with their furry companions.

We knew we had to break away from the monotony of our daily lives for quite some time before we decided to take off on a trip across the US and Canada. We were at our happiest when travelling, when exploring new places, when trying new foods, when immersing ourselves in new cultures. We thrive off experiencing new things and going on adventures. There is something magical about travelling; it goes beyond seeing different sights. It's the experiences that change you. We would come home from our trips, already ready to plan our next adventure, thirsty for another memorable experience.

Before we started our bus build, we were travelling every chance we had, but there was one thing really bothering us. We hated leaving our pets at home and missed them when we were away. We needed a way to continue to travel while still having them with us.

When we started our build, we had a dog and a cat. Having two pets was part of the reason we decided to convert a bigger bus instead of a van, so they would have a little more space. We only have a cat now. Our Labrador, Baxi, was diagnosed with cancer one month before

we planned to get on the road and her health declined rapidly after that. She didn't get to come on our bus journey, but she is forever in our hearts and we miss her so much. We will eventually continue our long-term travels abroad, but for now we plan on finishing the US and Canada with our buddy Mr Beebles and taking short trips abroad so we're not away from him for too long.

Since we were going to spend the next few years travelling in it, we wanted the bus to look and feel more like a tiny house than an RV. We love tiny homes and admire the lifestyle of those who live in them so we thought, 'why not build one on wheels?' We went to a few tiny house festivals and were very intrigued by the lifestyle. We even added an actual house door to give it that welcoming look. Another reason is that we wanted it to be completely off grid and customised to our needs. We have a wood-burning stove, real brick wall, completely solar, real quartz countertops, real tiles, real glass shower door and more. In addition to being a fully customisable blank canvas, school buses are the safest vehicles out there. They are the most regulated vehicles on the road according to the National Highway Traffic Safety Administration. RVs are not subject to the same rigorous safety crash tests as a school bus and cannot withstand an accident as well as a school bus can.

We had no experience with anything like this before starting the conversion, so we had to do a whole lot of research. We needed to take a lot of things into consideration so that the design didn't take away from the functionality and vice versa. They were both equally important to us. This took a tremendous amount of thought and time.

We haven't added up every single receipt, but we ended up spending close to around US$100,000 total on the build, give or take. The electrical system, including solar, batteries, inverter etc., was our most expensive luxury. We went with a pretty hefty setup. It is definitely a luxury not having to worry about power and not having to plug into shore power if we are in a remote area. It allows us to camp anywhere, worry free. Our biggest bargain was Robbie's natural skills for this type of thing. I designed it and he made it come to life! We saved a lot by doing the work ourselves. It would have cost us much more to hire a company to build it and it might not have turned out exactly how we wanted it.

We had many things go wrong and encountered many problems during the build, but it's all part of the process – along with finding solutions to them. We almost quit altogether three times! At one point we actually listed our gutted

bus online because our windows were leaking and we couldn't figure out how to stop the leak so we felt there was no way to continue. We tried everything including removing them, cleaning them and reinstalling them with new caulking, but they still leaked. The old seals had been dry rotted and water kept getting through even after we caulked over them. After some thought, we took down the listing and decided to get all new replacement windows. It worked! That was in the first couple of months.

We then ran into problems after we had completed the build. The bus was finished and we were extremely excited, but then we found out our engine had a blown head gasket and we needed a new one. The bus was in the shop for months, but we now have a new engine.

We love everything about our build and wouldn't change a thing. We built it just the way we wanted it. Our tiny wood-burning stove is definitely one of our favourite elements, especially on cold winter nights but we enjoy it as a focal point all year round as well. It has such a cosy and inviting look and feel to it.

Since converting our bus, we have been blessed with so many amazing opportunities, but the best one has been the ability to connect with people from all over the world who we have inspired with our story and travels. One time we were parked outside a grocery store in Montreal; when we got back to the bus, there was a note on our door from one of our followers inviting us for dinner at their house and welcoming us to park the bus on their land

while visiting their home town. You can't possibly feel more welcomed in a place than when experiencing something like this. We've always preferred learning from the locals when travelling and people's interest in our conversion has allowed us to experience this even more.

We have visited so many places that we absolutely love. In the US, Savannah (Georgia), Boston (Massachusetts) and the coast of Maine (Acadia National Park especially) are among our favourite places. In Canada, Cape Breton Island in Nova Scotia, specifically the village of Chéticamp, and Cape Breton Highlands National Park are at the top of our list on the East Coast.

Right now, we're back home in Florida and the bus is currently in storage. Our plan from the beginning was to travel the US and Canada with the bus and, after our last stop in Alaska, we planned on downsizing even more to a van in order to travel to other continents. The coronavirus pandemic changed our plans quite a bit with the closing of the Canadian border and travel becoming more of a challenge in general. It really slowed us down. We figured since the border was still closed and we had some downtime from travelling, we would build our van now and finish our trip in it instead of the bus. This means that when we're done with the west coast of Canada and Alaska, we can head to our next destination in the van without losing any additional time going back home to build the van. We started on our new van project in February 2021 and expect to be done in a few months. We're not sure what we will be doing with the bus just yet. We might sell it or possibly rent it out. Our first trip along the East Coast lasted ten months and we visited over 200 cities. This next trip will be continuous for a few years. It will be even more of an adventure, given that we will be officially living in the van full-time!

Follow Robbie, Priscilla and Mr Beebles' adventures on Instagram at going_boundless, as well as facebook.com/goingboundless and on their YouTube channel.

GOING BOUNDLESS

A renovated school bus that has been converted into a home is often called a skoolie.

Cost of conversion:	US$100,000
Biggest luxury:	The electrical system, but it means we don't have to worry about power.
Biggest bargain:	Robbie's skills and Priscilla's eye for design. That saved us having to hire a company to do it for us!
Biggest problem during build:	Stubborn leaking windows
Biggest problem after build:	Blown head gasket
Future plans:	Building our new van and continuing our travels in it with Mr Beebles.

WOTTIES VANLIFE

Mark and Alison emigrated from the UK to Australia in 2009, looking for a new lifestyle in the sun. After eight years of working hard and feeling dissatisfied, they looked into vanlife and started a new adventure.

Arriving in a new country was hard; we had left behind our support network of family and friends, as well as the old familiar places we knew. There wasn't the work promised and the cost of living was much higher than we'd been used to, but we managed. The first three years were hard, but with hard work and quite a bit of penny pinching we felt like we'd got somewhere, so we bought a house. I (Alison) ran my business from our converted garage and Mark had a full-time job in a joinery workshop about 10km from home, working from 6 a.m. till 2 p.m. or 4 p.m.; my job was full on, working 7 a.m. to 5 p.m. Monday to Friday. We were nearly eight years into this when we had our 'what are we going to do' chat. We just weren't enjoying our life, it was a slog and we didn't know what we were doing wrong. I know people will say, 'that's just the way it is, that's just life', but why does it have to be?

Our vanlife journey started here. Never in our wildest dreams did we think we would do this at our age, but luckily it has worked out well for us so far. We have met some wonderful people, made new friends and feel part of a rapidly growing community of vanlife warriors – those of us who dare to dream and throw caution to the wind.

Our story probably started in the same way many do, with the same question that many people ask at some point in their lives ask: Is this it? We couldn't see ourselves carrying on with our life the way it was. Don't get us wrong, we had a good life by most standards – we had a nice house, good jobs and were earning enough money to pay for the expenses with a little left over – but we never seemed to be able to afford to go on holidays without the fear of the bills piling up while we weren't earning as we were both self-employed. We were spending a lot of time working and very little quality time together, and the time we did find, we would often be too tired to enjoy it. It wasn't the way we wanted our lives to be. We felt very trapped in the same old week-in-week-out drudge and we couldn't see it changing unless we did something drastic. So we sat down and talked about what we could do. There were lots of different scenarios but none of them had the big change result we were looking for.

'We had to do some soul searching and work out what we really needed and what we could easily do without.'

We had been watching videos on YouTube for a while and had come across the vanlife movement; at first this just seemed like something young people or dreamers did, but the more we watched the more we realised maybe it could be the way forward for us. Fewer commitments meant less money needed, which meant less need to earn as much money, therefore we could work less, giving us more time together. It seemed drastic, but so was drifting apart and being bored with our lives. We had moved halfway around the world in our forties, we knew we could do almost anything if we stuck together. We were all in and decided to give it our best shot.

So the search for a van commenced in earnest. The choice of van was based mostly on size and cost, and after weeks of searching we finally found ours, a Renault Master LWB built in 2012, within our budget and seeming in good condition for its age. We decided to build our own van, making it just as we wanted and specific to our needs. Mark is a joiner by trade so the conversion would be built by him for the most part; I would be the interior designer and already had a vision of how the van would look and feel, choosing a colour scheme that reflected our love of the ocean and the beautiful blue skies of Australia. This build was 100 per cent a joint effort.

Our needs for our build were huge; we were moving out of a three-bedroomed house with all the usual modern conveniences and trying to fit everything that you think you need into such a small space was pretty mind-blowing. It was a lot to take in. We had to do some soul searching and work out what we really needed and what we could easily do without – or at least get used to being without. All of this requires a bit of a shift in your usual thinking. By watching vanlifers on YouTube, seeing how they lived, we learned the minimalist philosophy and saw just how little they needed to be happy and that really inspired us to go for it.

We didn't really write down a budget for the build, as we built it over twelve months, mainly at weekends; we just bought what we needed, when we needed it. If we couldn't afford something one week, we held off and got on with what we could. We didn't want to go into debt during the build, as getting out of debt was the reason for building it in the first place. We found some freebies along the way which certainly helped, in particular the pallet wood we used for the walls as well as some of the furniture – it's almost everywhere in our build. We got this for free, then all we did was paint, sand and varnish it to get the effect you can see inside the van. This look is very unique to us; we wanted the interior to reflect our personalities, our love for the rustic and the vintage look. Sadly, we didn't get a lot for free and some items were very expensive, the most expensive item being our Fiamma F65L awning which cost over $2,000 after being fitted – ouch! But we do use it quite often, so feel it was worth the money.

'We would highly recommend it to anyone, whatever your age or personal circumstances.'

We were, for the most part, incredibly lucky with our conversion with just a couple of hiccups along the way. Our first kitchen attempt just didn't work for us; looking back I don't think we really designed it with the 'living full-time' in it in mind. Our van wasn't finished 100 per cent, but we decided to try it out and go away for the Easter long weekend. Within one hour of sitting inside the van on a very rainy afternoon, we both knew it wasn't going to work. It was just too cluttered, with not enough storage and far too basic. So, it was back to the drawing board. Most vans are mostly kitchen, so it has to be 100 per cent for your own needs. Ironically, we are now on our third kitchen in nearly as many years.

We are always thinking of improvements for our vanlife journey, but really we only have a handful of items we might change should we re-build or build another van, the main one being that we would include a sofa and not have a fixed bed as we do now. We might look into a longer van with four-wheel drive in the future, so that every road is accessible for us to explore. We've been down some questionable roads and survived, but have passed by many others with regret, knowing we might not make it and would get stuck. On a recent visit to Waterfall Way in New South Wales during a very wet week, we got bogged down just on grass and in rural campground. With a four-wheel drive, we'd have been fine but there we were – wheels spinning, making a terrible mess of the landowner's grass and ourselves at the same time. We had to get out on our own as there was no one to help us; we used what we had, which just happened to be a tarp. We weren't hopeful and thought for sure we were stuck until the morning, but to our amazement putting the tarp under the front wheels and driving inch by inch for about 100ft allowed us to get out. We couldn't believe it worked – we were both dancing in the rain!

One of our most recent additions to our van has turned out to be one of our favourite parts of our build. We wanted to have more outside seating, without having to always get chairs out and sit beside our van, so we designed and built a pull-out 'Dickie' seat at the rear of our van. We have comfy cushions and small side tables on the inside of the rear doors for our beverages and it takes up no extra space within the van, which is a huge bonus. From this seat, we can sit comfortably and watch the sunset.

In Australia, we are very fortunate to be able to sit at the beach and watch dolphins play, whales and their babies swim past on migration or simply watch the world go by. There is no better pleasure, and it is one of the many reasons we enjoy vanlife. When we see wildlife, we often say, 'you don't see that sitting in your lounge, do you!' Our lives are so enriched by choosing this life, and we would highly recommend it to anyone, whatever your age or personal circumstances. The beauty of vanlife is that it is completely unique; you can make it whatever you want it to be, with whatever you have – cheap or

expensive, big or small van, or RV or car. The main thing is not to let your own limitations stop you, just start small. If you're not sure what to do, start with baby steps or go all in – it's up to you. Don't listen to the naysayers, make a choice for yourself and your own life. Yes, people are going to say, 'you're crazy!' We had the very same reaction when we told people we were selling our house, selling or giving to charity 80 per cent of our possessions to go and live in a 6.2m van. People just could not get their heads around the idea, but we did it anyway. We aren't out to prove anyone wrong. We all have our own path to tread, and this is ours right now, but who knows what is around the corner for us.

Our dream for our future is to be able to choose how to live our own lives without the rat race, to have fewer material possessions and feel free of the pressures of consumerism. Now we know how extraordinarily little we all really need to make us happy, we wonder why everyone doesn't do it. The end goal for us is to grow our YouTube channel and our online presence, and be able to work creatively on those, while travelling full-time and discovering more about this wonderful world and ourselves in the process.

Follow Mark and Alison's adventures on Instagram at wottiesvanlife and on their YouTube channel.

WOTTIES VANLIFE

Make of van:	2012 Renault Master LWB
Biggest luxury:	Fiamma F65L awning – but worth the money.
Biggest bargain:	The free pallet wood which is almost everywhere in our build.
Recent additions:	Our pull-out 'Dickie' seat to enjoy the sunset.
Future plans:	Growing our YouTube channel while learning more about this wonderful world!